Jihad in the Context of Contemporary Terrorism

– DIVERSITY OF PERSPECTIVES –

Mohamed Elamin
Elbushra Mahgoub

Jihad in the Context of Contemporary Terrorism

CONTENTS

ACKNOWLEDGMENTS

This research is a solicited work, and I would not have thought of writing it had it not been given support and encouragement by many participants of the 1st. Stockholm Criminology Symposium in 2006. I was given also an extraordinary encouragement from several Muslim scholars, whom I have contacted seeking explanations of the Quranic verses quoted in this work, historical events or to respond to my short questionnaire of this study. Although many of those scholars has requested, that their names should be withheld, I am very much in their debt, and looking forward for their further comments, critiques, and contributions in enhancing contemporary understanding of Islamic Jihad. I owe a debt of gratitude to the former professor of Keio University Koichi Miyazawa and his colleagues at the faculty of law. They reviewed and supported my first work on terrorism and criminal justice in 1988, drawing my attention to the links between Jihad and terrorism developed by western scholars. I should not forget Professor Tetsuya Ichii of Chiba University, advisor of my Japan foundation scholarship who supported me during my stay in Chiba University as visiting professor. Worthy to mention and appreciate Japanese television NHK channel for giving me an opportunity to understand new dimensions of terrorism through their interview questions to me.

At that early stage of terrorism history, professor Miyazawa and his colleagues were of opinion that social and political injustice should be emphasized as one of the probable causes of terrorism.

This study is not an attempt to give any Fatwa on Jihad or to develop any linkage between Jihad and terrorism, because Jihad is religious believe and worship for millions of Muslims throughout the world, while terrorism is a crime, unanimously denounced by the humankind. However, it may be impossible for non-Muslims to distinguish between Jihad or fighting for the Cause of Allah and terrorism, in the context of acts of violence prevailing today in many parts of the world with different causes.

El-Bushra

INTRODUCTION

Following the tragedy of September 11, 2001, that occurred in New York and Washington, which was linked, to a group of al Qaeda Mujahidin, Western scholars classified the study of Islamic Jihad as one of the most important disciplines to be examined. They began to review the relevant original sources of Islam in depth. Many efforts were made by those scholars to understand The Quran, holy book of all Muslims, looking for evidence that might support existing links between Islamic Jihad and the contemporary terroristic activities, if any. Several scholars and politicians went beyond that, to re-examine Islamic communities as a whole with the intention of understanding the reality of the cultures, knowledge, justice, equity, social welfare and political systems prevailing in those communities, as a probable cause of the growing trends of violence among Muslims first, and between Muslims and non-Muslims second.

On the other hand, Muslim scholars and politicians have condemned all patterns of the contemporary terrorism, and have repeatedly confirmed the fact that Islam is a religion of peace, mercy and justice. They are used to assert the innocence of Islam from any terrorist accusations. Muslim scholars routinely provide positive evidence from The Quran and other Islamic sources to support the quality of Islamic teachings and guidelines. However, Muslim scholars and politicians have never attempted to comment or thoroughly elaborate such evidence or Quranic verses related to Jihad and fighting for the Cause of Allah as pointed-out by non-Muslim scholars. It may be worthy to mention here that the original sources of Islam are known as:

Firstly: The Quran, which is the holy book revealed to Muhammed, and the Sunna which is the record of the sayings, doings, actions and explanations made by Prophet Muhammed.

Secondly: Complementary sources including;

1- The consensus of opinion
2- The analogy
3- Equity
4- Unspecified interests of the people
5- Avoidance of harm
6- Compatibility of the means and the ends
7- Checking what is permissible and what is prohibited.

The dilemma facing Muslim scholars and politicians, is not only to assure the quality of Islamic teachings, or to quote Quranic verses which are not readily visible in most of the Islamic communities of today. The real dilemma is to provide satisfactory explanations and a uniform concept of Jihad or fighting for the Cause of Allah based on such variable sources.

The challenge facing Muslim Scholars is adopting a common understanding on Jihad and Fighting for the Cause of Allah. It is urgent to determine whether Jihad or Fighting for the Cause of Allah is defensive or offensive, and to what extent.

Whom are the targets of Jihad and fighting for the Cause of Allah? How and who is responsible in managing Jihad and Fighting Affairs? What is the responsibility of the Islamic countries in managing Jihad and Fighting for the Cause of Allah, as far as they are obliged by the international laws? Does Jihad and Fighting for the Cause of Allah constitute a threat to International peace and security?

It is urgent to explain the phenomena of dissension and critical conflicts among the Muslims and within Islamic countries first. It is essential to understand causes of the growing terroristic trends within Islamic communities, particularly among new generations. How can we face and rebut the allegations and religious slogans of the contemporary Jihad leaders spreading among the Muslims?

Muslim scholars, who attempt to advocate excellence of Islam as a religion, always tend to quote attractive examples of the early history of Islam. They continuously detail, how Prophet Muhammed and his companions and followers has treated non-Muslims, and how they established peaceful communities and realized justice before fourteen centuries. Such historical evidence and quotations are well known by many Western scholars. Therefore, such evidence may not be admissible before non-Muslims, who are witnessing horrible examples and life practices among the Muslims and within the Islamic countries. Muslim scholars, politicians, leaders and individuals are urged to establish within their communities and political systems a new and visible examples that might be credited to Islam.

Surly, Islam denounces terrorism and condemns killing innocent people. Islam has forbidden violence and use of force within the communities. It encourages peace between people and nations. This is well known to the Western circles at all levels, therefore, they are raising the question "Why Muslims of today are different?"

This study provides an outline for the concept of Jihad and Fighting for the Cause of Allah from the perspective of the Muslim scholars and non-Muslim scholars. The intention of this study is inviting, or even provoking Muslim scholars to provide well established defense and come together with a uniform response that might create a favorable environment for all Muslims first, and for the human being second. This study is an attempt to:

- Enhance the adoption of a uniform understanding of Islamic Jihad and Fighting for the Cause of Allah with its identified dimensions and targets, as a religious worshiping to be respected by all parties.
- Enforce such understanding among the Muslims first, by Islamic teachings and legislative means, and within the global community second, by means of an international law.

- Provide an unanimously acceptable explanation of the Quranic verses related to Jihad and Fighting for the Cause of Allah, in the context of the contemporary global environment.
- Underline available Quranic and Sunna evidence that might nullify any allegations against Jihad and Fighting non-Muslims in the context of the contemporary thinking of western scholars.
- Finally, to determine how far Islamic Jihad and Fighting for the Cause of Allah is a religious worshipping, and does not constitute any form of threat or terror for non-Muslims.

By highlighting the controversial opinions of Muslim and non-Muslim scholars, this study may provide grounds to distinguish between Islamic Jihad and contemporary terroristic activities and political violence. Considering Jihad and terrorism as a concern of the international community, the study aims suggesting new ideas and practical tools to adopt a global framework for peace and justice, that might lead to prevention of terrorism and identify the roots and the future of culture conflict threatening global peace and security.

ONE

THE SCOPE OF ISLAMIC JIHAD

1. Defining Jihad

Jihad is an Arabic word from the basic verb form "juhd" meaning effort. Other forms of this verb are "jahada", "Mujahid" and "Ijtihad". Jihad means to strive, endeavor or put one's utmost efforts and power, whether physically, mentally or by any inner means, to perform a definite task. In the context of Islamic thought, Jihad means to strive, struggle or fight in Allah's cause. Two concepts of Jihad can be identified in Islamic teachings and juridical literature:

1) the minor Jihad, which is fighting against the enemies of Islam to defend and spread the Islamic religion. This type of Jihad should be conducted under the guidance of the political authorities and according to the needs of the Islamic nations.

2) the greater Jihad, which is the task of self-containment of every Muslim to prevent himself from doing wrong or spreading sin. In a primary sense, this type of Jihad is an inner thing, within the self, to rid the person of debased actions or inclinations, and to strive to meet good standards. Since Islam is not confined to the boundaries of the individual but extends to the welfare of the societies and humanity in general, an individual cannot

keep improving himself/herself in isolation from what happens in his community or in the world at large. In this sense, Jihad is a duty which is not exclusive to Muslims but also applies to the human race in general, as shown in the Quran:

"And strive hard in Allah's cause as you ought to strive, he has chosen you and has not laid upon you in religion any hardship. It is the religion of your father Abraham. It is he who has named you Muslims both before and in this Qur'an" (22:78).

At its most literal meaning, Jihad- sometimes is called the "sixth pillar of Islam"[1]- It is cognate with words such as "endeavor" and "effort". As such, it may be applied to almost any kind of striving, individual or collective, that accords with Islamic principle. To qualify as an architect and aim to build a mosque, or to construct a dam where it will benefit members of the Islamic community or realize justice and peace are examples of Jihad. For instance, in Islamic Republic of Iran, the campaign for reconstruction and building the country after the war was undertaken by an organization called "construction Jihad". In this sense Jihad is a sort of selfless social duty. Yet, in a profound sense, Jihad considered as warfare was and is secondary. Indications of Jihad might have a nonviolent meaning are cited in the following:

"A member of fighters came to the messenger of Allah, and he said: You have done well in coming from the minor Jihad to the greater Jihad. They said, what is the greater Jihad?

He said "For the servant of Allah to fight his passions" is the greater Jihad.

---

1 The unanimously agreed upon five pillars of Islam are:
  To admit that there is no God but Allah and Muhammed is his Messenger (shahadah).
  Performing prayers five times a day (salat).
  Giving alms to poor and needy people (Zakat)
  Fasting during the month of Ramadan (sawm)
  Making a pilgrimage to Mecca (hajj)

Caliph Umar, returning from a visit to the front line against Byzantium, famously declared that warfare was the "minor Jihad". The "greater Jihad" was to build a just and equitable society amongst those who already swore obedience to Allah.

According to the unanimous opinion of Muslim jurists, Al-Jihad in Allah's cause, with full force of numbers and weaponry, is given the utmost importance in Islam. Jihad is one of the pillars on which Islam stands. By Jihad Islam is established, Allah's Word is made superior, and his religion is propagated. By abandoning Jihad, Islam may be destroyed and Muslims may fall into an inferior position; they may lose their honor, land and holy places.

In Islam, Jihad is a fundamental element of belief, worshipping and even cause of life. Jihad is an obligatory duty on every Muslim. It is not just a temporary duty performed to face a state of emergency or a sudden aggression, but it is a permanent and continuous effort of preparedness to maintain a powerful Islamic Community capable of both existing and practicing its principal duties in this life, which is to worship Allah.

Ibn Tymmiya considers Jihad as a means to realize what Allah loves from belief and good behavior, and the repulsion of what Allah hates such as disbelieving, incontinence and contempt. Jihad, for Allah's cause, is not only fighting for Allah's cause by hands and weapons, but also through other means such as speeches, teaching others and calling people to Islam... etc. Jihad may be by the heart, maintaining positive intentions and feelings, and that is why the Prophet Muhammad carried out his mission by inviting people to Islam for thirteen years. Fighting for the Cause of Allah was not in practice at the beginning of Muhammad's mission; however, it was permitted later, and finally was made obligatory against:

1- Those who fight Muslims or their religion.
2- Those who worship others except Allah.
3- Those who expel Muslims unjustly from their homeland.

"March forth whether you are light (being healthy, wealthy and young) or heavy (being old, ill and poor) and strive hard with your wealth and your lives in the cause of Allah. This is better for you if you but knew" (9:41).

It is most obvious that, Jihad is the fighting against disbelievers and the enemies of Allah's messenger. Therefore, anyone who has received the messenger's call for Islam, but rejected it should be fought, so as not to become bewitched, and so that all religion becomes for Allah. Muslims must fight any one who obstructs their efforts in bringing about Islamic teachings.

According to the Shafiya school, Jihad is fighting for Allah's cause,[2] whilst in the Malikiya school Jihad is fighting by Muslims against disbelievers to bring out Islam. But according to the Hanafiya school the concept of Jihad is wider. It includes fighting for Allah's cause by words, property or self-sacrifice

The means to fulfil this sense of Jihad are varied, and in the modern word encompass all legal, diplomatic, arbitral, economic, and political activities. However, it is important to note that Islam does not exclude the use of force to curb evil, if there is no other workable alternative. Indeed, a forerunner of the collective security principle and collective intervention to stop aggression, outlined in the United Nation's Charter, is the Quranic reference "...make peace between them (the two fighting groups), but if one of the two parties persists in aggressions against the other, fight the aggressor until they revert to Allah's commencement". The sense of 'greater Jihad', therefore, means that military action is a sub element of what is meant by Jihad, but not its totality. That was what Prophet Muhammed emphasized to his companions when returning from a military campaign, when he told them: "this day we have returned from the minor Jihad (war) to the major Jihad (self-control and betterment)."[3]

The subject of Jihad has been discussed with particular emphasis and in considerable details in the Quran. There is consensus of opinion amongst Muslim scholars, that no other action has been explained in

---

2　بدائع الصنائع : الكاساني، عام 1997.

3　ابن المبارك: كتاب الجهاد.

such great detail as Jihad. Allah has revealed many Quranic Verses primarily to guide the believers towards this path. The subject of Jihad has been expressed in many different ways, in numerous verses of the Qur'an. The verses explain in detail the clear objectives and benefits of Jihad. The status of the Mujahid is honored in the Quran and there are many verses which warn of the danger of abandoning Jihad. There is such a great emphasis of this subject, that some commentators and scholars of the Quran have remarked that the core of the Quran is Jihad. The terminology of Jihad-Fi-Sabilillah, which means Jihad in the Path of Allah, has been used in the Quran twenty-six times and the specific word, Qitaal (Fighting), used in the context of fighting in the Path of Allah, is mentioned in the Quran seventy-nine times. There are whole Chapters in the Quran, which have been revealed, explaining the rule and virtues of Jihad and admonishing those ignoring Jihad; such as Surah Anfal. There are Chapters in Quran which are named after battles, clearly illustrating rules of fighting and management of the battlefield and guidelines of the victory[4].

In the Sunnah there are thousands of Ahadith or the Prophetic reports regarding Jihad. The experts in the field of Hadith) have compiled the sayings and actions of the Prophet relating to Jihad, which clearly give evidence to the importance of Jihad in Islam[5(1)].

The definition of Jihad in Shari'ah Terminology: "Exhausting the utmost effort fighting the disbelievers to make Allah's religion the highest"; is comprehensive and restrictive. It is comprehensive because it includes the linguistic meaning of Jihad and the attributes of Jihad.

---

4 **See the following sources:**
Holly Quran, Chapters: 2, 4, 5, 9, 27, 30, 33, 48, 57, 100, 110.

5 **See the following sources:**
Sahih Bukhari Consists of 241 chapters under the title of Jihad (p34-275, vol.4).
Sahih Muslim Consists of 100 chapters under the title of Jihad (p942-1063, vol.3).
Tirmizi Consists of 115 chapters under the title of Jihad (p282-302, vol.1).
Abu Dawood Consists of 172 chapters under the title of Jihad (p342-362, vol.2).
Nasai Consists of 48 chapters under the title of Jihad, (p53-66, vol.2).
Ibne Majah Consists of 46 chapters under the title of Jihad, (p197-207).

It is restrictive since it involves fighting only the disbelievers for the sole purpose of raising Allah's name.

There is difference of opinion as to whether Jihad is only an offensive duty or whether it can be attributed to both offensive Jihad and defensive Jihad. Al Izz Ibnu Abdul Salaam (known as Sheikh al Jihad) said that it is only an offensive duty not defensive i.e. Jihad by definition will only be called so if we initiate fighting, the other duty (i.e. defensive Jihad) is called Al Dafa'ah. Defending oneself being instinctive in man just as it is with the animals, not a unique duty like offensive Jihad.

Moreover, Ibnu Qayum laid down certain conditions for Jihad:

i)   That the Muslims must start or initiate the fighting.
ii)   That the fighting must be against the disbelievers fighting the apostates is called Qaatal al Ridda, as an implementation of the Islamic penal code; whilst fighting the rebels is called Qaatal al Baghee, neither of these being Jihad.
iii) Al Ma'niyyah - having the intention of fighting to make Allah's religion dominant, which is not usually the case in defensive Jihad, since one usually fights for victory or martyrdom, but not looking to implement the Islamic ruling system in such circumstances.

Therefore, there are two divisions of Jihad:

i)   Al-Jihad al-Mubadahah - Offensive Jihad.
ii)   Al-Jihad al-Dafa'ah- Defensive Jihad.

However since linguistically the word Jihad connotes the exhaustion of effort, it is found used within the Quran with different meanings e.g. self-Jihad etc.. When Allah describes fighting as Jihad He uses the word Qital and one who fights is called Muqatil.

Imam Shafi said that the reason why Muslims fight the disbelievers (offensive Jihad) is that they reject religion of Islam and are at war with it. Imam Abu Hanifa on the other hand said that Muslims should fight the disbelievers (offensive Jihad) because:

i)   They fight Muslims, and

ii) They reject Islamic religion to be implemented.

Offensive Jihad can only be carried out by the Islamic state. There are three stages, which lead to Jihad. Firstly, the people are invited to embrace Islam. If they refuse to become Muslims, then they are requested to become citizens of the State (Dhimmis) and are asked to pay Jizya (a small tax). If even this is refused, then the state declares war upon them.

Defensive Jihad is an obligation upon the Muslim whose life, honor and wealth are under aggression. They are asked by Allah to fight and protect themselves. Thus this type of Jihad may be carried out without the existence of an Islamic state. Therefore, the foreign policy of the Islamic State may be offensive Jihad.

The purpose of offensive Jihad is to remove any obstacle in the way of implementing the laws of Islam. In other words, the implementation of the Islamic law, the Sharia is of utmost importance to Muslims. The Sharia is a comprehensive system of life, covering all aspects of life to govern humanity. It is the only just way to live, as it is from the Creator Allah. Whether Muslim or non-Muslim, the state would protect the life, honor and wealth of a person[6].

In Islam, material benefit is not what motivates Muslims to carry out the command of Jihad, rather it is obeying and submitting to Allah.

The Islamic ideology is an ideology revealed by Allah. It offers the only correct, comprehensive, and viable way of life for the human being, providing him with a sound purpose, a clear vision, and a stable life. It manifests itself in the personalities of its followers and in the form of a system implemented by a State. It is a universal ideology meant to liberate all of humanity. Consequently, one cannot accept for this ideology to be confined to a specific people or land; rather, it has to be offered to all of humanity. In order to deliver this ideology to the rest of humanity, the State that adopts this ideology shoulders the responsibility of carrying it to new lands. As would be expected,

---

6 www.ummah.net/forum/showthread.php?t=22388

this goal will lead to a conflict with other states and their ideologies. This conflict has to be resolved either through diplomacy or through force. Every ideology utilizes these alternatives. All leading nations use diplomacy and force.

Several Muslim scholars attempted to defend Jihad by saying that, the term Jihad, cannot be translated as 'holy war', nor can it be translated, as the word 'struggle'. At best, its legal meaning can be understood as "using military force, where diplomacy fails, to remove the obstacles the Islamic State faces in carrying its ideology to mankind". Therefore, aim of Jihad, in the past, was not to forcibly convert the inhabitants of other lands to Islam. However, it was to provide them with the security that comes from the application of Islam, leaving them the choice of adopting Islam or keeping their own religions. According to Muslim scholars, Islamic state in Spain where Muslims, Christians, and Jews were able to live peacefully under an Islamic authority is suggested as a historical positive evidence. It was the Islamic justice that allowed non-Muslims in the Islamic State to flourish as artisans, writers, and thinkers.

2. History of Jihad

Since Allah's messenger Muhammed began preaching and calling people to Islam in the year 612, many threats were made against his life. Some of Mohammed's followers were assaulted or killed, others were forced to migrate persecution by the disbelievers in Mecca. However, Muhammed and his followers never attempted to use force or struggle to defend themselves. They continued to preach and invite people to Islam peacefully for thirteen years, because Muhammed was not ordered by Allah to use force; on the contrary, he was asked during that period to spread Islam with wisdom and fair preaching and argument.

> *"Invite mankind to the way of your lord with wisdom and fair preaching. And argue with them in a way that is better. Truly, your lord knows best who has gone astray from his path"* (8:125).

After the first thirteen years of peaceful preaching, the Quranic verses permitting fighting (Jihad) – only as self-defense – were revealed. Thereafter, Quranic verses, gradually outlined the rules and principles governing Islamic fighting (Jihad). Finally, Islamic Jihad became a religious duty and a matter of worship for every Muslim. Jihad as such was a significant factor in leading the Islamic armies to many victories over well organized and experienced armies in the Sassanian and Byzantine empires. From the Quran, and from what we know of the political context of the time, we may infer that typical Islamic Jihad is that which was performed between the years 624 and 661. During or at the end of the era of the fourth caliph in the year 661, political unrest began to spread within the Islamic state. Thereafter, Islamic warfare became largely internal and increasingly inconsistent with the basic rules of Jihad. Although this may be a matter of some controversy, we may assert that Jihad (fighting for Allah's cause) may only be declared or authorized by caliphs, imams, emperors or sultans of an Islamic state. However, in the absence of an Islamic political entity or head of state, the right to declare "Jihad' becomes much more problematic.

The collapse of the Ottoman empire in the 1918 is cited as the end of the first Islamic state founded fourteen centuries earlier in Arabia. That State extended its territorial jurisdiction over many parts of Asia, Africa and Europe. At the Allies conference of 1919 at Versailles, the Arab and Islamic nation was re-tailored by the victorious powers of the 1st. world war, in line with the Sykes-Picot agreement of 1916, giving the current political and geographical boarders and definitions of the Arab and Islamic countries. The newly tailored countries were occupied by British, Russian, French and Italian forces.

Consequently, since 1919, there has been no single united Islamic state. Instead, there are now several states inhabited by majority of Muslims. However, given that calling for Jihad lies only within the jurisdiction of the head of the Islamic state, it is not possible to envisage a legitimate Jihad being called, because of the absence of an appropriate Islamic authority to declare or sponsor Jihad.

During the twentieth century, the so called Islamic countries have witnessed internal fighting and armed struggle for independence.

However, the term Islamic Jihad has never been used to describe such fighting, except in Palestinian war of 1948, when individual Muslims were allowed to travel and fight in Palestine against Israel, but not as organized governmental armies. Even the Iranian Shi'ite revolution of 1979, led by Ayatollah Khomeini, which deliberately sought to establish an Islamic society, never attempted to declare any form of Islamic Jihad to overthrow the former Iranian Shah. That was mere political upraise. Moreover, the kingdom of Saudi Arabia, the only country governed by sharia, has never since it was established by the late king Abdul Aziz Al-Saud in 1932, attempted to declare or authorize Islamic Jihad, for any purpose. Therefore, the notion of Jihad -as minor Jihad- had almost ceased to exist in the Muslim world after the 10th. Century, until it was revived with the American encouragement in Afghanistan to expel the Soviet out that country.

We may conclude the history of Jihad by focusing the fact that; during the last three or four decades, there have been only two ambiguous situations where Islamic Jihad was sponsored directly or indirectly by a government or governmental organization:

1) in 1979, following the Soviet occupation of Afghanistan, Afghan guerrillas fought to expel their invaders. However, this was not just an ordinary war of national resistance. It came to be regarded as a global Islamic Jihad, waged by mujahidin or 'holy warriors, whose numbers were swelled by Arab, African, Pakistani, Muslim Chinese, and even American, Indonesian and Filipino volunteers. Eventually worn down by continuing conflict, the Russians withdrew in 1989, and a great Islamic Jihad victory was proclaimed. Yet the mujahidin had only triumphed with the aid of the United States of America and its allies channeled through Pakistan. It might be thought that the outcome was in fact a triumph for Washington: America had fought a surprisingly successful proxy war that accelerated the breakup of its ideological enemy, the Soviet Union, mainly by employing the notion of Jihad and benefiting Muslims believe

in Jihad. The victorious Islamic Jihad against the former Soviet Union two controversial critical facts:

a) It developed tremendous confidence among the Muslims and generated sufficient evidences of religious miracles known in Islamic literature.

b) It provided lessons to America and the West, showing that Jihad notion is a powerful threat, and probable to extend to defeat the West by any aid from China or the former Soviet Union.

2) in 1990, the Sudanese government sponsored Islamic Jihad to control the military insurgency in the Southern and Eastern parts of Sudan. Many Muslims from Norther Sudan went on Jihad in the Southern part of the country, supported by several Islamic groups from abroad. Although that pattern of so-called Jihad has led to a peaceful settlement of a long war, it might be classified as a political fighting rather than Jihad. However, it should be noted that in both of the above situations, although they were initially cited as Jihad, they were later rejected by many scholars and Muslims, including its planners, such as Sheikh Hassen Al-Turabi, due to it is well known objectives and outcomes.

3. Sources and principles of Jihad

There are more than forty verses in The Quran calling for Jihad and showing the most valuable rewards waiting those who maintain Jihad for Allah's cause; but those Quranic verses has classified Jihad into two types, namely general and special Jihad as follows:

1. The general Jihad

The Quranic verses commanding Muslims to preform general Jihad are:

- *Surah Al- Furqan: "So obey not the disbelievers, but strive against them (by preaching) with the utmost endeavor with it (the Quran)"* (25:52)

In this text, Jihad does not refer to fighting, but it emphasizes only preaching, teaching others and explaining Quran for the people.

- *"And those whosoever strives, he strives only for himself. Verily, Allah stands not in need of any of the mankind, Jinn and all that exists"* (29:6)

Again, this is another evidence of greater Jihad by striving for oneself, but for the cause of Allah who is not in need of man or jinn to maintain his word.

- *"And strive hard in Allah's Cause as you ought to strive with sincerity and with all your efforts that His Name should be superior. He has chosen you to convey His Message of Islamic Monotheism to mankind by inviting them to His religion of Islam, and has not laid upon you in religion any hardship: it is the religion of your father Ibrahim"* (22:78).

This Quranic verse emphasizes striving with peaceful and sincere means, and not by fighting. In this context, Jihad is urgent to perform all religious obligation. Therefore, fasting and pilgrimage are considered the best form of Jihad.

2. The special Jihad:

There are many forms of special Jihad, the most important one is to endeavor and sacrifice with one's self. Due to the seriousness of this type of "Jihad" the Quran outlines its causes and rules in several verses as follows:

- *"But if they violate their oaths after their covenant, and attack your religion with disapproval and criticism, then fight you the leaders of disbelief (chiefs of Quraish pagans of Makkah) for surely, their oaths are nothing to them — so that they may stop evil actions"* (9:12).

- *"Will you not fight a people who have violated their oaths pagans of Makkah and intended to expel the Messenger while they did attack you first, Do you fear them? Allah has more right that you should fear Him if you are believers"* (9:13).

- *"Fight against them so that Allah will punish them by your hands and disgrace them and give you victory over them and heal the breasts of a believing people,"* (9:14).

- *"And remove the anger of their hearts. Allah accepts the repentance of whom He wills. Allah is All-Knowing, All-Wise"* (9:15).

- *"Do you think that you shall be left alone while Allah has not yet tested those among you who have striven hard and fought and have not taken, advisors and consultants from disbelievers, pagans giving openly to them their secrets, besides Allah and His Messenger, and the believers. Allah is Well-Acquainted with what you do"* (9:16).

- *"Do you consider the providing of drinking water to the pilgrims and the maintenance of Al-Masjid Al-Haram as equal to the worth of those who believe in Allah and the Last Day, and strive hard and fight in the cause of Allah? They are not equal before Allah. And Allah guides not those people who are the wrongdoers"* (9:19).

The above two Quranic verses have asked the Messenger to fight the disbelieving people of Makkah. If that was the concept of fighting during the Prophetic era, shall we take fighting disbelievers as an everlasting obligation? a question remains a waiting an answer.

- *"Those who believed in the Oneness of Allah and emigrated and strove hard and fought in Allah's cause with their wealth and their lives are far higher in degree with Allah. They are the successful"* (9:20).

- *"Fight against those who believe not in Allah, nor in the Last Day, nor forbid that which has been forbidden by Allah and His Messenger and those who acknowledge not the religion of truth among the people of the Scripture (Jews and Christians), until they pay the Jizyah with willing submission, and feel themselves subdued"* (9:29).

- *Verily, the number of months with Allah is twelve months, so was it ordained by Allah on the Day when He created the heavens and the earth; of them four are sacred (the 1st, the 7th, the 11th and the 12th months of the Islamic calendar). That is the right religion, so wrong not yourselves therein, and fight against the pagans, and disbelievers in the Oneness of Allah, collectively as they fight against you collectively. But know that Allah is with those who are the pious"* (9:36).

- *"O you who believe! What is the matter with you, that when you are asked to march forth in the cause of Allah (i.e. Jihad) you cling heavily to the earth? Are you pleased with the life of this world rather than the Hereafter? But little is the enjoyment of the life of this world as compared to the Hereafter"* (9:38).

- *"March forth. Whether you are light or heavy, and strive hard with your wealth and your lives in the cause of Allah. This is better for you, if you but knew"* (9:41).

- *"Those who believe in Allah and the Last Day would not ask your leave to be exempted from fighting with their properties and their lives; and Allah is the All-Knower of the pious"* (9:44).

- *"O you who believe! Fight those of the disbelievers who are close to you, and let them find harshness in you; and know that Allah is with those who are pious".* (9:123)

- *"Let those believers who sell the live of this world for the Hereafter fight in the cause of Allah, and whoso fights in the cause of Allah, and is killed or gets victory, We shall bestow on him a great reward"* (4:74).

- *"And what is wrong with you that you fight not in the Cause of Allah, and for those weak, ill-treated and oppressed among men, women, and children, whose cry is: "Our Lord! rescue us from this town whose people are oppressors; and raise for us from You one who will protect, and raise for us from You one who will help"* "(4:75).

- *Those who believe, fight in the Cause of Allah, and those who disbelieve, fight in the cause of Satan. So fight you against the friends of Satan; ever feeble indeed is the plot of Satan" "(4:76).*

- *"Not equal are those of the believers who sit at home, except those who are disabled, and those who strive hard and fight in the cause of Allah whith their wealth and their lives. Allah has preferred in grades those who strive hard and fight with their wealth and their lives above those who sit at home. Unto each, Allah has preferred those who strive hard and fight, above those who sit by a huge reward" "(4:95).*

- *"Think not of those who are killed in the Way of till when you have killed and wounded many of them, then bind a bond firmly. Thereafter is the time either for generosity (i.e. free them without ransom), or ransom (according to what benefits Islam), until the war lays down its burden. Thus you are ordered by Allah to continue Allah as dead. Nay, they are alive, with their Lord, and they have provision" (3:169).*

- *"They rejoice in what Allah has bestowed upon them of His Bounty and rejoice for the sake of those who have not yet joined them, but are left behind that on them no fear shall come, nor shall they grieve" (3:170).*

- *"So, when you meet in fight—for Allah's Cause, those who disbelieve, smite their necks till when you have killed and wounded many of them, then bind a bond firmly. Thereafter is the time either for generosity or ransom, until the war lays down its burden. Thus you are ordered by Allah to continue in carrying out Jihad against the disbelievers till they embrace Islam and are saved from the punishment in the Hell-fire or at least come under your protection], but if it had been Allah's Will, He Himself could certainly have punished them. But He lets you fight in order to test some of you with others. But those who are killed in the Way of Allah, He will never let their deeds be lost" (47:4).*

- *"And surely, We shall try you till We test those who strive hard for the Cause of Allah and the patients, and We shall test your facts who is a liar, and the one who is truthful" (47:31).*

- "And fight them until there is no more Fitnah polytheism, or worshipping others besides Allah and the religion will all be for Allah Alone. But if they cease worshipping others besides Allah, then certainly, Allah is All-Seer of what they do" (8:39).

- "And make ready against them all you can of power, including steeds of war to threaten the enemy of Allah and your enemy, and others besides whom, you may not know but whom Allah does know. And whatever you shall spend in the cause of Allah shall be repaid unto you, and you shall not be treated unjustly" (8:60).

- "O Prophet Urge the believers to fight. If there are twenty steadfast persons amongst you, they will overcome two hundred, and if there be a hundred steadfast persons they will overcome a thousand of those who disbelieve, because they are people who do not understand" (8:65).

"Now Allah has lightened your task, for He knows that there is weakness in you. So if there are hundreds they shall overcome two hundred, and if there are a thousand of you, they shall overcome two thousand with the Leave of Allah. And Allah is with the patient" (8:66).

"Verily, those who believed, and emigrated and strove hard and fought with their property and their lives in the cause of Allah as well as those who gave them asylum and help, - these are all allies to one another. And as to those who believed but did not emigrate to you O Mohammad, you owe no duty of protection to them until they emigrate, but if they seek your help in religion, it is your duty to help them except against people with whom you have a treaty of mutual alliance; and Allah is the All-Seer of what you do" (8:72).

- "And fight in the Way of Allah those who fight you, but transgress not the limits. Truly, Allah likes not the transgressors (1:190). "And kill them wherever you find them, and turn them out from where they have turned you out. And Al-Fitnah is worse than killing. And fight not with them at Al-Masjid-Al-Haram, unless they first fight you there. But if they attack you, then kill them. Such is the recompense of the disbelievers" (1:191).

- *"Jihad is ordained for you Muslims though you dislike it, and it may be that you dislike a thing which is good for you and that you like a thing which is bad for you. Allah knows but you do not know.*[7](1) (1:216)

The Quranic verses where the term Jihad was used in particular may be interpreted as greater Jihad which emphasizes the spiritual efforts, abandoning sins and binding oneself to Islamic teachings, however, the verses directly calling for fighting may never be interpreted otherwise. Such verses are:

* *"And fight in the Way of Allah and know that Allah is All-Hearer, All-Knower."* (2:244)
* *"And fight in the Way of Allah those who fight you, but transgress not the limits. Truly, Allah likes not the transgressors.* (2: 190)
* *"And kill them wherever you find them, and turn out from where they have turned you out. And Al-fitnah is worse than killing. And fight not with them at Al-Masjid – Al-Haram, unless they fight you there. But if they attack you, then kill them. Such is the recompense of the disbelievers."* (2: 191)
* *"Let those believers who sell the life of this world for the Hereafter fight in the cause of Allah, and who so fights in the cause of Allah, and is killed or gets victory, We shall bestow on him a great reward."* (4: 74)
* *"And what is wrong with you that you fight not in the cause of Allah, and for those weak, ill-treated and oppressed among men, women, and children, whose cry is – our lord rescue us from this town whose people are oppressors; and raise for us from you one who will protect, and raise for us from you one who will help"* (4:75)
* *"But if they violate their oaths after their covenant, and attack your religion with disapproval and criticism then fight (you) the leader of disbelief (chiefs of Quraysh pagans of them Makkah)- for*

---

7 Interpretation of the Meaning of the Noble Quran, summarized version of Al-Tabari, Al-Qurtubi and Ibn Kathir. By Muhammad Taqi-Udin Al-Hilali and Muhammad Muhsin Khan.

surely, their oaths are nothing to them – so that they may stop evil actions." (9: 13)

*   *"Will you not fight a people who have violated their oaths (pagans of Makkah) and intended to expel the Messenger while they did attack you first? Do you fear them? Allah has more right that you should fear him if you are believers." (9:13)*

*   *"Fight against them so that Allah will punish them by your hands and disgrace them and give you victory over them and heal the breasts of a believing people" (9:14)*

*   *"Verily, the number of months with Allah is twelve months (in a year), so was it ordained by Allah on the Day when he created the heavens and the earth; of them four are Sacred (i.e. the 1ˢᵗ, the 7ᵗʰ, the 11ᵗʰ, and the 12ᵗʰ months of Islamic calendar). That is the right religion, so wrong not yourselves therein, and fight against the Mushrikun (polytheists, pagans, idolaters, disbelievers in the Oneness of Allah) collectively as they fight against you collectively. But know that Allah is with those who are AL-Muttaqun." (9: 36)*

The merits of Jihad and fighting in the cause of Allah are extensively highlighted by the Sunna – Prophetic reports – however, it is essential to refer in this context to the most sound authenticated Prophetic reports which are known as the Divine Hadith:

*   …I would like to be killed a lot of times for the cause of Allah (Al - Bokhary, part 1 page 16)

  - As the struggling for the cause of Allah is as the fasting the standing in prayers; Allah promised the struggler if he dies, the paradise as the reward and if he does not, he will come back with a wage or a plunder (Bokhary, part 5, page 36).

  - Allah promised the fighter, if he dies, the paradise as the reward and if he does not; he will come back soundly with a wage or a plunder (Al-Nissai, part 1, page 16).

  - Allah the Glorified did vouch who struggles for the cause of Allah, when he goes to Jihad with his intent for Allah, no one else, for paradise or to return him back to his own home that he goes out of it with what he gains from wage or plunder. (Al-Nissai, part 1, page 16).

- Allah says to Shaheed: ask and wish. Shaheed says: I ask you to return me back to the lifetime because I would like to be killed for the cause of Allah ten times, that is due to what he finds of the merits of martyrdom. (Al – N issai, part 1, page 37).

- …I order you to do five things as Allah ordered me: togetherness, listening, obeying, immigration and Jihad in the cause of Allah. (Bukhary, 1720).

- … The tourism of my nation is Jihad in the cause of Allah. (Sahih Al-Jamei, 2089)

Bearing in mind, the importance of Quran as the most irrevocable and everlasting holy reference of all Muslims, and source of their teachings and behavior, we can summarize the permanent rules and facts affirmed by the above-quoted Quranic verses of Jihad as follows:

1. The Quran exhorts Muslims to take part in Jihad, and has made clear the rewards for those who perform Jihad.
2. "Mujahidin" are the troops of Allah who will establish Islam, and repel the might of His enemies and protect Islam and guard the religion safely.
3. "Mujahidin" should fight against the enemies of Allah in order that worship should be only for Allah and that Islam should be superior.
4. 4- Quran commands Muslims to fight against all disbelievers as well as the scriptures (Jews and Christians) if they do not embrace Islam until they pay the taxes levied on them, provided that they are under an Islamic government.
5. Believers performing Jihad are superior before Allah than those believers who are performing other kinds of worship.
6. Jihad as fighting in Allah's cause was forbidden at the beginning of Prophet Muhammad's mission, then it was permitted and later it was made obligatory against:

- Those who start fighting against Muslims, but not against those who did not fight them.
- All those who worship others along with Allah.
- Those who unjustly expel Muslims from their homes.

7. Those who lead, invite, and abet others for Jihad and support "Mujahidin" with wealth and weapons are also given equal rewards as Jihad doers.
8. To prepare well trained troops and maintain weapons and strong fighting forces is obligatory[8]. Therefore, Muslims have no reason to abandon Jihad.

4. Future of Jihad and Qittal

In general, Jihad as the sixth pillar of Islam will remain in the hearts of all believers in Muslim communities until the Day of Resurrection. Self-sacrificing for the cause of Allah, who has ordained Jihad, will remain as a dream for every Muslim to be rewarded with lofty dwellings in Paradise. Existence of Jihad in the hearts of Muslims includes intentions, feelings, speeches and Daawa or call for Islam, and performance of righteous deeds. Therefore, it is duty of Muslim scholars to clarify the concept of Jihad in the concept of international law and the global peace and security policies.

Here, there is a reasonable interaction between Daawa and Jihad. Daawa combined with Jihad as two complementary strategies. Daawa needs efforts and special weapons including religious knowledge and personal skills. Daawa objectives are as follows:

- Correction of the belief of people and their thought on Allah.
- Speaking about the concept of the Muslims' universal role and function.

---

8 In this context many Muslim scholars consider Nuclear weapons as one of the sources of force to be procured by Muslims to the extent that this weapon is procured by their enemies.

- Directing people to worship Allah and eradicate all other forms of belongings.
- Track corruption and injustice on the earth with the intention of its eradication.
- Continuous call for the right religion.

Therefore, Daawa can be focused as a peaceful means of Jihad; however, it is the ultimate introduction to the minor Jihad which is fighting for the cause of Allah by all means. The reality of the greater Jihad and Daawa is that it strengthens the individual Muslim and the Muslim Community as well. If the whole social settings are converted into righteous Islam, the community will be a striving community "Mujtama Mujahid".

Probably Jihad should be constructive social activities and humanitarian services benefiting humanity, through modern understanding, whenever Muslim scholars arrive to acceptable consensus. However, the future Qittal or fighting for the Cause of Allah stated in The Quran may remain as debatable issue. It is most essential for Muslim scholars to adopt unanimously acceptable interpretations for fighting –related Quranic verses, such as the following verses:

> *2:190 And fight in the Way of Allah. Those who fight you, but transgress not the limits. Truly, Allah likes not the transgressors. (This Verse is the first one that was revealed in connection with Jihad, but it was supplemented by another (9:36)).*

> *2:191 And kill them wherever you find them, and turn them out from where they have turned you out. And Al-Fitnah is worse than killing. And fight not with them at Al-Masjid-Al-Haram (the sanctuary at Makkah), unless they (first) fight you there. But if they attack you, then kill them. Such is the recompense of the disbelievers.*

2:193 And fight them until there is no more Fitnah (disbelief and worshipping of others along with Allah) and (all and every kind of) worship is for Allah (Alone). But if they cease, let there be no transgression except against Al-Zalimun (the polytheists, and wrong-doers).

2:194 The sacred month is for the sacred month, and for the prohibited things, there is the Law of Equality (Qisas). Then whoever transgresses the prohibition against you, you transgress likewise against him. And fear Allah, and know that Allah is with Al-Muttaqun (the pious.)

2:216 Jihad (holy fighting in Allah's cause) is ordained for you (Muslims) though you dislike it, and it may be that you dislike a thing which is good for you and that you like a thing which is bad for you. Allah knows but you do not know.

2:218 verily, those who have believed, and those who have emigrated (for Allah's religion) and have striven hard in the Way of Allah, all these hope for Allah's Mercy. And Allah is Oft-Forgiving, Most-Merciful.

2:244 And fight in the Way of Allah and know that Allah is All-Hearer, All Knower.

2:246 Have you not thought about the group of the Children of Israel after (the time of) Musa (Moses)? When they said to a Prophet of theirs, appoint for us a king and we will fight in Allah's Way." He said, "Would you then refrain from fighting, if fighting was prescribed for you? They said, "Why should we not fight in Allah's Way while we have been driven out of our homes and our children (families have been taken as captives)?" But when fighting was ordered for them, they turned away, all except a few of them. And Allah is All-Aware of the Zalimun (polytheists and wrong- doers).

3:157 And if you are killed or die in the Way of Allah, forgiveness and mercy from Allah are far better than all that they amass (of worldly wealth).

3:169 Think not of those who are killed in the way of Allah as dead. Nay, they are alive, with their Lord, and they have provision.

3:170 They rejoice in what Allah has bestowed upon them of his Bounty and rejoice for the sake of those who have not yet joined them, but are left behind (not yet martyred) that on them no fear shall come, nor shall they grieve.

3:195 So their Lord accepted of them (their supplication and answered them), "Never will I allow to be lost the work of any of you, be he male or female. You are (members) one of another, so those who emigrated and were driven out from their homes, and suffered harm in My Cause, and who fought, and were killed (in My Cause), verily, I will expiate from their evil deeds and admit them into Gardens under which rivers flow (in Paradise); a reward from Allah, and with Allah is the best of rewards.

4:74 let those (believers) who sell the life of this world for the Hereafter fight in the Cause of Allah, and is killed or gets victory, We shall bestow on him great reward.

4:75 And what is wrong with you that you fight not in the Cause of Allah, and for those weak, ill-treated and oppressed among men, women, and children, whose cry is "Our Lord! Rescue us from this town whose people are oppressors; and raise for us from You one who will protect, and raise for us from You one who will help.

4:76 Those who believe, fight in the Cause if Allah, and those who disbelieve, fight in the cause of Taghut (Satan). So fight you against the friends of Shaitan (Satan); ever feeble indeed is the plot of Shaitan (Satan).

4:84 Then fight (O Muhammad) in the Cause of Allah, you are not tasked (held responsible) except for yourself, and incite the believers (to fight along with you), it may be that Allah will restrain the evil might of the disbelievers. And Allah is Stronger in Might and Stronger in punishing.

4:91 You will find others that wish to have security from you and security from their people. Every time they are sent back to temptation, they yield thereto. If they withdraw not from you, nor offer you peace, nor restrain their hands, take (hold of) them and kill them wherever you find them. In their case, We have provided you with a clear warrant against them.

4:95 Not equal are those of the believers who sit (at home), except those who are disabled (by injury or are blind or lame), and those who strive hard and fight in the Cause of Allah with their wealth and their lives. Allah has preferred in grades those who strive hard and fight with their wealth and their lives above those who sit (at home). Unto each, Allah had promised good (Paradise), but Allah has preferred those who strive hard and fight, above those who sit (at home) by a huge reward.

5:35 O you who believe! Do your duty to Allah and fear Him. And seek the means of approach to Him, and strive hard in His Cause (as much as you can), so that you may be successful.

5:54 O you who believe! Whoever from among you turns back from his religion (Islam), Allah will bring a people whom He will love

And they will love Him; humble towards the believers, stern towards the disbelievers, fighting in the Way of Allah, and never afraid of the blame of the blamers. That is the Grace of Allah which He bestows on whom He wills. And Allah is All-Sufficient for His creatures' needs, All-Knower.

8:49 And fight them until there is no more Fitnah (disbelief and polytheism, i.e. worshipping others besides Allah) and the religion (worship) will all be for Allah Alone (in the whole of the world) But if they cease (worshipping others besides Allah), then certainly, Allah is All-Seer of what they do.

8:60 And make ready against them all you can of power, including steeds of war (tanks, planes, missiles, artillery) to threaten the enemy of Allah and your enemy, and others besides whom, you may not know but whom Allah does know. And whatever you shall spend in the Cause of Allah shall be repaid unto you, and you shall not be treated unjustly.

8:65 O Prophet Muhammad Urge the believers to fight. If there are twenty steadfast persons amongst you, they will overcome two hundred, and if there be a hundred steadfast persons they will overcome a thousand of those who disbelieve, because they (the disbelievers) are people who do not understand.

8:72 Verily, those who believed, and emigrated and strove hard and fought with their property and their lives in the Cause of Allah as well as those who gave (them) asylum and help, - these are (all) allies to one another. And as to those who believed but did not emigrate (to you O Muhammad), you owe no duty of protection to them until they emigrate, but if they seek your help in religion, it is your duty to help them except against a people with whom you have a treaty of mutual alliance; and Allah is the All-Seer of what you do.

8:74 And those who believed, and emigrated and strove hard in the Cause of Allah (Al-Jihad), as well as those who gave (them) asylum and aid these are the believers in truth, for them is forgiveness and Rizqun Karim (a generous provision i.e. Paradise).

8:75 And those who believed afterwards, and emigrated and strove hard along with you (in the Cause of Allah), they are of you. But kindred by blood are nearer to one another (regarding inheritance) in the decree ordained by Allah. Verily, Allah is the All-Knower of everything.

9:5 Then when the Sacred Months (the 1ˢᵗ, 7ᵗʰ, 11ᵗʰ and 12ᵗʰ months of the Islamic calendar) have passed then kill the Mushrikun wherever you find them, and capture them and besiege them, and lie in wait for them in each and every ambush. But if they repent and perform As-Salat (Iqamat-as-Salat), and give Zakat, then leave their way free. Verily, Allah is Oft-Forgiving, Most Merciful.

9:12 But if they violate their oaths after their covenant, and attack your religion with disapproval and criticism then fight (you) the leaders of disbelief (chiefs of Quraysh pagans of Makkah)- for surely, their oaths are nothing to them- so that they may stop (evil actions).

9:13 Will you not fight a people who have violated their oaths (pagans of Makkah) and intended to expel the Messenger while they did attack you first? Do you fear them? Allah has more right that you should fear him if you are believers.

9:14 Fight against them so that Allah will punish them by your hands and disgrace them and give you victory over them and heal the breasts of a believing people.

9:19 Do you consider the providing of drinking water to the pilgrims and the maintenance of Al-Masjid Al Haram (at Makkah) as equal to the worth of those who believe in Allah and the Last Day, and strive hard and fight in the Cause of Allah? They are not equal before Allah. And Allah guides not those people who are the Zalimun (polytheists and wrongdoers).

9:20 Those who believed (in the Oneness of Allah- Islamic Monotheism) and emigrated and strove hard and fought in Allah's Cause with their wealth and their lives are far higher in degree with Allah. They are the successful.

9:24 Say: If your fathers, your sons, your brothers, your wives, your kindred, the wealth that you have gained, the commerce in which you fear a decline, and the dwellings in which you delight… are dearer to you than Allah and His Messenger and striving hard and fighting in His Cause, then wait until Allah brings about His Decision (torment). And Allah guides not the people who are Al-Fasiqun (the rebellious, disobedient to Allah).

9:29 Fight against those who (1) believe not in Allah, (2) nor in the Last Day, (3) nor forbid that which has been forbidden by Allah and His Messenger (Muhammad) (4) and those who acknowledge not the religion of truth (i.e. Islam) among the people of the Scripture (Jews and Christians), until they pay the Jizyah with willing submission, and feel themselves subdued.

9:38 O you who believe! What is the matter with you, that when you are asked to march forth in the Cause of Allah (i.e. Jihad) you cling heavily to the earth? Are you pleased with the life of this world rather than the Hereafter? But little is the enjoyment of the life of this world as compared to the Hereafter.

9:39 If you march not forth, He will punish you with a painful torment and will replace you by another people; and you cannot harm him at all, and Allah is Able to do all things.

9:41 March forth, whether you are light (being healthy young and wealthy) or heavy (being ill, old and poor), and strive hard with your wealth and your lives in the Cause of Allah. This is better for you, if you but knew.

9:44 Those who believe in Allah and the Last Day would not ask your leave to be exempted from fighting with their properties and their lives; and Allah is the All-Knower of Al-Muttaqun (the pious).

9:73 O Prophet (Muhammad) Strive hard against the disbelievers and the hypocrites, and be harsh against them, their abode is hell, -and worst indeed is that destination.

9:86 And when a Surah (chapter from the Quran) is revealed, enjoining them to believe in Allah and to strive hard and fight along with His Messenger, the wealthy among them ask your leave to exempt them (from Jihad) and say, "Leave us (behind), we would be with those who sit (at home)."

9:88 But the Messenger (Muhammad) and those who believed with him (in Islamic Monotheism) strove hard and fought with their wealth and their lives (in Allah's Cause). Such are they for whom are the good things, and it is they who will be successful.

9:111 Verily, Allah has purchased of the believers their lives and their properties for (the price) that theirs shall be the Paradise. They fight in Allah's Cause, so they kill (others) and are killed. It is a promise in truth which is binding on Him in the Taurat (Torah) and the Injeel (Gospel)

9:122 And it is not (proper) for the believers to go out to fight (Jihad) all together. Of every troop of them, a party only should go forth, that they (who are left behind) may get instructions in (Islamic) religion, and that they may warn their people when they return to them, so that they may beware (of evil).

9:123 O you who believe! Fight those of the disbelievers who are close to you, and let them find harshness in you; and know that Allah is with those who are Al-Muttaqun.

16:110 Then, verily, your Lord-for those who emigrated after they had been put to trials and thereafter strove hard and fought (for the Cause of Allah) and were patient, verily, your Lord afterwards is Oft- Forgiving, Most Merciful.

22:39 Permission to fight (against disbelievers is given to those (believers) who are fought against, because they have been wronged; and surely, Allah is Able to give them (believers) victory-.

22:40 Those who have been expelled from their homes unjustly only because they said: "Our Lord is Allah". For had it not been that Allah checks one set of people by means of another, monasteries, churches, synagogues, and mosques, wherein the Name of Allah is mentioned much would surely, have been pulled down. Verily, Allah will help His (cause). Truly, Allah is All-Strong, All-Mighty.

29:6 And whosoever strives, he strives only for himself. Verily, Allah stands not in need of any of the Alamin (mankind, jinn, and all that exists).

30:69 As for those who strive hard in Us (Our Cause), We will surely, guide them to Our Paths (i.e.) Allah's Religion-Islamic Monotheism). And verily, Allah is with the Muhsinun (good doers).

47:31 And surely, We shall try you till We test those who strive hard (for the Cause of Allah) and As-Sabirun (the patient), and We shall test your facts (i.e. the one who is a liar, and the one who is truthful).

61:4 Verily, Allah loves those who fight in His Cause in rows (ranks) as if they were a solid structure.

62:11 That you believe in Allah and His Messenger (Muhammad), and that you strive hard and fight in the Cause of Allah with your wealth and your lives: that will be better for you, if you but know!

66:9 O Prophet (Muhammad)! Strive hard against the disbelievers and the hypocrites, and be severe against them; their abode will be Hell, and worst indeed is that destination.

73:20: He knows that there will some among you sick, others traveling through the land, seeking of Allah's Bounty, yet others fighting in Allah's Cause. So recite as much of the Quran as may be easy (for you), and perform As-Salat (Iqamat-as-Salat) and give Zakat, and lend to Allah a goodly loan. And whatever good you send before you for yourselves, you will certainly find it with Allah, better and greater in reward. And seek Forgiveness of Allah. Verily, Allah is Oft-Forgiving, Most-merciful.

When interoperating the above-mentioned verses, it may be essential for all Muslims to know and be satisfied with the answers of the following questions:

1. Who are the disbelievers (Kafiroon) of today to be fought and killed?
2. When shall such fighting be declared and by whom?
3. How far Muslims are obligated to fight throughout the world for the Cause of Allah?
4. Are Muslims obliged to fight and kill those who verbally criticizes Islam or obstruct spreading it in the world?

Consequently, we may outline the following scenarios for the future of Jihad:

1. If Muslim communities remain under the present unfavorable political and social circumstances, Jihad may easily be converted by extremists into violence and terrorism from time to time causing unpredictable damages for the mankind.

2. If Muslim communities are developed by all means and became a strong nation, capable to face the Non-Muslim Nations, they will surely fulfill all religious requirements of Jihad to the end and until Allah's word becomes superior.

3. If Muslim communities are developed carefully and fairly through mutual understanding with Non-Muslim Communities enabling new generations to live in free societies maintaining their cultural identity governed by internal laws, peace may prevail throughout the world.

TWO

GAUGING INTERNATIONAL TERRORISM

1. Understanding terrorism:

Despite attempts made by many academic scholars and the experts of the United Nations to define terrorism, no one definition for the term has gained universal acceptance. The many political and ideological pressures of the last century were no doubt in part responsible for this. However, for the purpose of this study, we may consider the elements of this crime within the following most popular definitions:

1. According to Schmidt: "Terrorism is a method of combat in which random or symbolic victims serve as an instrumental target of violence. These instrumental victims share group or class characteristics which form the basis for their selection for victimization. Through pervious use of violence or the credible threat of violence, other members of that group or class are put in a state of chronic fear (terror). This group or class, whose members' sense of security is purposefully undermined, is the target of terror.[9(1)]

---

9 Schmidt, quoted in Shukri, Ibid., P. 2.

2. An updated definition by Bassiouni, which was accepted by the United Nations' Interregional Committee in 1988, reads as follows: "(Terrorism is) an ideologically motivated strategy of internationally proscribed violence designed to inspire terror violence within a particular segment of a given society in order to achieve a power-outcome or to propagandize a claim or grievance irrespective of whether its perpetrators are acting for and on behalf of themselves or on behalf of a state'.[10(1)]

3. Hudson defines terrorism as: "A sudden, unexpected act of shocking, calculated, and unlawful violence, or the plausible threat of group usually carried out in a peaceful, civilian or against certain noncombatants or targets that represent or symbolize a certain country, but sometimes indiscriminately against bystanders or passerby at a particular location, with the intention of garnering publicity, propagandizing a cause and intimidating as many people as possible in order to attain social, political, or strategic objectives.[11(2)]

4. The United States' code, title 22, section 2656 (f) defines terrorism as follows:
    - The term "terrorism" means premeditated, politically motivated violence perpetrated against noncombatant targets by sub-national groups or clandestine agents, usually intended to influence an audience.
    - The term "international terrorism" means terrorism involving citizens or the territory of more than one country.
    - The term "terrorist group" means any group practicing, or that has significant subgroups that practice, international terrorism.

These definitions are accepted by the Muslim scholars, who unanimously condemn such terrorism activities. There is no doubt

---

10 Mahmood Sherif Bassiouni, United Nations' Intergovernmental Meetings of the Experts, Vienna, 14-18 March 1988.

11 Rex A. Hudson "Dealing with International Hostage Taking Terrorist, Volume No. 221, London, 1983.

among Muslims, that all forms and patterns of killing of innocents is prohibited and severely punishable. However, it must also be noted that there are several scholars who tend to look at foreign occupation as a reasonable cause and right for fighting by all means, including all forms of terroristic activities, including suicide terrorism against random victims.

2. History of terrorism

Terrorist organizations appeared for the first time in ancient history during the first and fourth century. At the forefront of these organizations were two organizations that are very similar to the contemporary terrorist organizations in terms of their goals, secrecy, and suicide operations, namely;

- Organization of Zealots Judea, which was known to the Romans as the Invisible Man. The members of this organization were assassinating members of the Roman army and their Jewish collaborators.
- Organization of Assassins, which was a group that broke away from the Shiites and took its headquarters in northern Iran, and its goals were to assassinate the leaders of the enemy with suicide operations [1].

During the period from the fourteenth century to the seventeenth century, terrorism and brutality were widely used during wars and conflicts, but the brutal terrorist operations of that stage did not bear the characteristics of contemporary terrorism. That type of terrorism ended with the emergence of the Nation-State system with the adoption of the Treaty of Westphalia in 1648. Recorded history indicates that, the French Revolution adopted the term "terror" in 1795 for the first time. The agents of the Security and Safety Committee were the first to use terrorism to control citizens. Terrorism also used opponents of the French Revolution to assassinate agents of the security services of the French Revolution. The Paris public played a major role in carrying out terrorist operations before, during and after the French Revolution, especially in assassinations that were carried out on senior officials and aristocrats.

In the nineteenth century, radical political theories appeared. The emergence of these theories was accompanied by a development in weapons technologies, providing an environment for the emergence of small revolutionary groups that attack the Nation-State and carry out assassinations among its political leaders. These revolutionary terrorist organizations have achieved some gains and public acceptance. Among the assassinations carried out by these radical organizations were the assassinations of the heads of governments in Russia, France, Spain, Italy, and the United States of America. However, poor cooperation and integration of such organizations with the local communities made them expire without causing any political effects. On the contrary, revolutionary terrorist organizations were replaced by communist organizations that used ideological political terrorism among the masses, achieving outstanding results in the twentieth century. The growth of communism ideology was accompanied by the emergence of organizations that demanded liberation and struggle against colonialism and the search for their own national identity.

One of the most prominent terrorist organizations that formed a model was the Russian organization known as "Narodnya Volya", meaning the will of the people. This organization appeared in 1878 in the Russian city of Leningrad and one of its terrorist operations was assassination of Tsar Alexander II in 1881 and the bombing of a dining hall in the Tsar palace in 1880 in addition to the assassination of a number of senior Russian officials[2].

In the seventies of the twentieth century, terrorism became international. The term international terrorism became popular for the first time in 1968 when the Popular Front for the Liberation of Palestine developed hijacking tactics, precipitating the hijacking of the Israeli El Al plane flying from Rome to Tel Aviv on 22nd. July 1968.

In the late twentieth century was the disintegration of the eastern camp and the end of the republic of the Soviet Union and the sole control of the world became under the western camp led by the United

States. At that time, the terrorist organizations of a nationalist struggle retreated. Some of them turned to religious terrorist organizations, to appear on the scene with extremist religious terrorist organizations such as Al-Qaeda and the various Jihadist organizations. Thus, the terrorist operations reached their most modern form represented by the Islamic State, Jabhat Al-Nusra, Hezbollah, the Houthis, and Boko Haram, which transferred their operations from the stage of suicide bombings to the stage of tactical wars.

Contemporary terrorism has been accompanied by a new form of terrorism known as cyber terrorism where modern technologies of information and electronic communications have become a weapon in the hands of some well-known and secret terrorist organizations. Evidence suggests that cyber terrorism began with the Gulf War in / 1991 and used in the conflicts in Haiti, Serbia, Russia, Syria, Iraq and Iran and has achieved decisive results in some of those disputes [3].

In the first half of the twentieth century, the world witnessed two world wars. Humanity placed its hopes on the results and data of the two wars in establishing a global legal system that guarantees people security and peace and suffices with the scourge of wars. However, freedoms at the same time ignited the spirit of patriotism and love of freedom in all parts of the world, which moved national organizations calling for resistance and revolution against foreign occupation. As these organizations took a racist and ethnic character, they found support from international politics. Some of those organizations have chosen the path of violence and terrorism in escalating their demands and rights. Peaceful civilians became a target and affected by the operations of those terrorist organizations, which succeeded in achieving their goals through terrorism, such as the Irish organizations, but some of them failed, such as the Macedonian organizations.

The Soviet Union at that stage contributed in supporting terrorist organizations based on the aforementioned demands, and that was in the context of the cold war between the eastern and western camps. [4].

The following is a list of the most famous terrorist organizations known throughout history :

- Assassins
- Sicari
- Socialist and communist organizations
- Badermenhof Group, renamed the Red Army
- Popular Front for the Liberation of Palestine

Italian Red Brigade
- Greek revolutionary struggle
- The Brilliant Path of Al-Biruni
- Spanish Eta Basque
- Irish IRA
- PKK Kurdish
- Sri Lankan Tamil growth
- Al-Qaeda
- Aum Shinryuko Japanese
- American Chloe Kicks
- Filipino Abu Sayyaf Group
- Palestinian Hamas
- Lebanese Hezbollah
- Palestinian Islamic Jihad Organization
- Egyptian Islamic Jihad Organization
- Al Nusra
- ISIS
- Houthis
- Boko Haram

This historical background documented in studies, research and international references confirms that terrorism is a phenomenon like ordinary crimes that has haunted societies since man knew living in a group.

The conflicting interests of societies, the different goals and objectives, the security and political variables, the economic needs and the sources of natural resources are all factors that make the doors of terrorism, violence and regional wars open. Such a phenomenon that is deeply rooted in human history cannot be said to be eradicated by such theoretical and propaganda attempts put forward by contemporary societies, their security services and the measures of their international system.

Terrorism is originally a pattern of deviation from the public order and the prevailing political reality. It is a difference of opinion and thought that did not find acceptance within the societies or the states to confront the argument with the argument and the opinion with the others opinion, through peaceful exchange of statements, clarifications and evidence between the two parties. The outlaws of public order may be less patient and less open to the requirements of reality, but societies and the majority must bear the opinions of the hypocrites and be patient to convince them of the right means, without resorting to violence and confronting by controversial security measures.

The violation of public order and the adoption of violence by some minorities is natural, as it is difficult for the general public to unanimously agree on an opinion on permanent basis through times and ages. Therefore, eliminating terrorism completely is one of the impossible things. However, the vital lesson to be considered is preventing and minimizing the cases of outlaws of the prevailing political, social and economic systems by pre-emptive partnership in all administrative, social and economic processes.

Islamic societies are the most experienced in breaking the prevailing regimes and using violence and terrorism. Muslims witnessed terrorism and violence in the early days of Islam, starting with the assassination of the greatest leaders and the most just and fair, learned and honest rulers of the world such as the Rightly Guided Caliphs Omar Ibn Al-Khattab, Othman and Ali.

The Muslims also witnessed the disagreements of the Kharijites, the Mu'tazila, and other Islamic groups that came out against the consensus of Muslims and formed organizations that have had negative effects up to date.

From here, we can say that the Arab countries need to pause carefully about the phenomenon of terrorism, understand it and evaluate it, taking into account the historical background of terrorism and violence, especially within the Arab countries, before jumping to the security measures that have proven to be unsuccessful.

Confronting terrorism in the Arab countries needs transparency and credibility in expressing opinions and freedom of dialogue with oneself and the other. Confronting terrorism and talking about violence in Arab countries is a peculiar affair that other countries of the world do not have in common.

2.3 Stages of the development of terrorism

Terrorist crimes and tactical wars have become an inherent phenomenon of ancient and contemporary societies. It is a phenomenon that advances and regresses in its size and dimensions according to the political, social, economic, regional and international changes. Whatever is around us vindicating the arena of governments and peoples, we find ourselves in front of evidence confirming the existence of hidden fingers of governments and peoples that directly or indirectly contribute to the movement, harnessing and exploitation of terrorist groups for their own agendas. If this covert support, assistance and exploitation is limited in the traditional terrorist crimes, however, it has become more clearly and powerfully contributing in the contemporary terrorist crimes, which we call tactical wars. Heavy weapons, advanced devices, equipment, means of transportation and smart electronic communications are only evidence of qualified sources and destinations that support terrorist groups and stand behind them strongly.

The traditional terrorist groups that emerged in the early twentieth century had clear political demands. They were trying to attract the attention of the world that neglected those demands. However, it is difficult to discern clear and convincing political motives for the tactical war groups of today, which are spilling blood, destroying homelands and defeating religious values and beliefs, they claim.

By reviewing traditional terrorist activities and tactical warfare, we can divide them into three main stages:

The first stage: the stage of terrorism justified by political and liberation demands:

This phase extended from the sixties to the nineties of the twentieth century. The terrorist operations at this stage had supporters who saw them as a heroic struggle for deserved human rights, as they had opponents. Studies indicate that (80%) of the terrorist organizations for this stage have been eliminated through security operations or political settlements, and (10%) of these organizations have been able to achieve their goals.

The second stage: the stage of al-Qaeda:

This phase began with various Jihadist organizations that received the support of Western intelligence and were used to fight the Soviet Union and expel it from Afghanistan. After the expulsion of the Soviet forces, Afghanistan became a hotbed of terrorism of the second stage, with an extremist Islamic character.

With the Mujahidin emerging from the cloaks of Western intelligence and their declaration of Jihad against Western countries, terrorist operations entered a new, more powerful and violent phase, as it provided them with land, mechanisms, and advanced devices that they inherited from the developed countries.

The terrorism of this stage, after the unification of most of its organizations under the leadership of Osama bin Laden, continued to enjoy the support of some Islamic countries and religious groups.

The terrorist operations of this stage were the cause of tactical wars similar to the world, which led to disasters in the Middle East and the Near East, which ended with the wars of Afghanistan and Iraq led by the United States of America and its allies with unclear goals and incorrect reasons that were proven invalid. Those wars brought about limited political changes, but they deepened the wounds and established sustainable terrorism and chaotic political and military activities that led the region to the worst.

The third stage: the stage of tactical wars:

It is the most dangerous stage experienced by the Arab and Islamic countries in the Middle East. We say that they are tactical wars because they are organized wars that move on a wide geographic scale, occupy lands, establish governments and manage the economy, but they are anonymous and the real goals are.

Fighting groups have moved from more than a hundred countries of the world to parts of Iraq, Libya and Nigeria, declaring their allegiance to the Islamic State and working with it to fight and commit atrocities against humanity. Groups that violate international law and custom and commit war crimes in their worst forms, control natural resources, export them, and benefit from their revenues in purchasing weapons, food, and the latest information and communication technologies for more than two years.

So, the terrorism of today is not the terrorism of yesterday. The tactical wars waged by terrorist organizations have no geographical boundaries and extend from the Near and Middle East to Africa. These organizations move with organized forces, advanced mechanisms, and modern devices and equipment. These organizations confront the great powers and withstand their air strikes. Above all, it directs targeted strikes in Western countries using the traditional methods of terrorism represented in specific terrorist operations based on secrecy and suicide bombings.[5].

This gradual development of terrorism in its various forms and forms was accompanied by a development in the seizure of loss of life and property and the horrific patterns of terrorist operations and terrorist practices.

According to statistics for the year 2015 the number of victims of international terrorism increased at the level of the year by (80%) as the highest rate of increase in the number of victims of the phenomenon of terrorism. While the financial cost of terrorist losses amounted to (52.9) billion US dollars.

Among the most important features of these statistics are the following:

- Terrorism killed (32,658) people in 2014 compared to (18,111) people in 2013, recording the highest rate of increase.
- Boko Haram and the Islamic State (ISIS) killed (51%) of the victims.
- Boko Haram topped the list of the most bloodshed terrorist groups.
- (78%) of the victims and (57%) of the terrorist attacks were concentrated in five countries: Afghanistan, Iraq, Nigeria, Pakistan and Syria.
- Iraq came as the country with the highest number of terrorism deaths, with a number of (99,929) people during the year 2014.
- The number of deaths in Nigeria reached (7512) in 2014, an increase of (300%) over the year 2014.[6]
- In 2001, the US security lists of terrorists were (16) names. In 2013, this number jumped to (469,000) names and reached (680000) names in 2015.

Terrorism is not a new phenomenon. It is deeply rooted in the history of the mankind and the use of terror and psychological warfare to intimidate and de-stabilize other communities has roots in antiquity. Since the early Bronze age and the rise of barbaric tribes who conquered agricultural communities and drove them off the land to live in walled cities, terror has been a significant weapon in man's effort to dominate.[12]

Terrorism as a criminal phenomenon has been documented at least since the 1st century. It was originally a barbaric way of life and turned into religious activity, until it became secular only with the French revolution, which offered terror a nationalist aspect. By the end of 19th century, the assassination of heads of states had become a means for terrorists to effect revolutionary, political and social changes and a number of kings, presidents and ministers were murdered between 1865 and 1905.

Contemporary international or intra-state terrorism, with its different forms, is a strategy and methodology of struggle between

---

12 Baring, A. and J. Cash ford, the Myth of the Goodness, London: Viking, 1991.

communities with diverse political, ethnic, cultural and religious backgrounds. As Darwin set out in his theory: "...the development of living things depends on the conflict and struggle. The strong win the struggle. The weak are condemned to defeat. There is a ruthless struggle for survival and eternal conflict in nature"[13]. If this is the case, it seems that terrorism will remain. World history moves from catastrophe to catastrophe, and between 1945 and 1990, there were approximately seventy-five serious conflicts throughout the world.

Such data, mapping terrorist activities suggests the incidence is rising. According to the Stockholm International Peace Research Institute (31) conflicts were counted for the year 1994, while the National Defense council foundation counted (71) conflicts in 1995.[14] Recently issued Japanese Ministry of self-defense report has pointed to (115) areas of conflicts and crisis on the world map[15]. The following is a chronological list of significant documented terrorist activities:

- In 1900, the assassination of German ambassador in Beijing and the king of Italy marked new phase of terror.
- In 1945 and 1946, the Jewish terrorist offensive against British rule bombed railways, oil refineries, and offices of the British government in Palestine.
- In 1950s, the Irish Republican Army emerged as a terrorist force in Northern Ireland.
- In the 1960s, the first American airliners were hijacked to Cuba, and the Palestinians began to commit terrorist acts of resistance to Jewish rule in the occupied territories.
- In the 1970s, the Baeder-Meinhof gang of West Germany, the Red Army of Japan, the Red Brigades in Italy, the Al-Fatah in Palestine, and the Shining Path of Peru emerged as potent terrorist groups.

---

13 Harun Yahya, The Real Ideological Root of Terrorism-Darwin and Materialism. www.harunyahya.com

14 Max Taylor and john Horgan, the future of terrorism, London: rank cass, 2000.

15 Japanese Defense Agency, Defense of Japan, Tokyo, Urban Connections, 2000.

- By the beginning of the 1980s, terrorists and guerilla movements were active on most continents of the world, and the scope of terror expanded to include acts of mass violence
- In the 1990s, kidnaping for large ransoms occurred with greater frequency throughout Central America and South America. The World Trade Center was bombed for the first time in 1993, killing six people and injuring over 1,000. The Aum Shinrikyo doomsday cult released sarin nerve gas into the Tokyo subway in 1995, killing twelve people and injuring 5,500. The bombing of the Federal Building in Oklahoma City killed 268 in 1995. In 1996, the Khoper Towers were bombed in Dhahran, Saudi Arabia, killing nineteen United States military service members. In 1998, suicide bombers simultaneously attacked United States Embassies in Tanzania and Kenya, killing 224 people, including twelve Americans.
- In 2000, seventeen sailors were killed and thirty-nine injured when a U.S. Naval ship, the U.S.S. Cole, was bombed in the port of Aden in Yemen.
- In 2001, four transcontinental airliners were hijacked and subsequently crashed—two into the World Trade Center in New York, one into the Pentagon in Washington DC, and the fourth into the central Pennsylvania countryside in a single coordinated terrorist act that left over 3,000 people dead or missing
- The U.S. Department of State currently profiles 106 terrorist groups active on the continents of North America, South America, Europe, Africa, and Asia.
- In an analysis of acts of international terrorism occurring in 2001, the U.S. Department of State (BPA 2002) reported that there were:
  - o 253 bombings (including the attacks on the World Trade Center).
  - o 41 armed attacks.
  - o 36 kidnappings.
  - o 3 hijackings...

- The U.S.A Department of State reported that of the 4,655 casualties of internationalism terrorism in 2001, 277 were members of the government, 25 were members of the military, and 4,353 were civilians.

The statistical data, maintained by the bureau of public affairs, U.S. department of state since 1960s, reveals that, the total number of international terrorist incidents were almost in decrease. However, the number the number of fatalities, injuries and financial losses are increasing, as well as the growing state of fear among the general public, as detailed in the following table.

Statistics on International Terrorism

Year	International Terrorism		
	Incidents	Fatalities	Injuries
1968	124	34	191
1969	189	55	110
1970	300	128	161
1971	241	35	91
1972	528	147	166
1973	323	120	504
1974	429	304	690
1975	349	258	556
1976	468	406	805
1977	428	245	299
1978	544	438	405
1979	441	686	1060
1980	499	486	332
1981	489	164	1187
1982	500	129	637
1983	506	641	1045
1984	565	329	502

1985	635	816	1255
1986	612	591	1221
1987	665	623	1219
1988	605	643	1131
1989	375	411	420
1990	437	218	366
1991	565	102	242
1992	363	91	636
1993	431	109	1393
1994	322	314	663
1995	440	177	6291
1996	296	314	2911
1997	304	221	693
1998	274	741	5953
1999	395	233	706
2000	426	405	800
2001	355	3295	2283
2002	205	725	2013
2003	208	625	3646
2004	651	1907	9000
2005	660	813	1065

Source: U.S. Department of State.

3. Analyses of Terrorism

In 1999 Lesser in his Introduction to the Rand publication 'Countering the New Terrorism' [16] made the point that our ways of thinking about terrorism needed change. He was particularly critical of the focus by students of terrorism on individual terrorist groups, and because of that what he described as their failure to '…characterize the

---

16 Lesser, I.O., Hoffman, B., Arquilla, J., Ronfeldt, D.F., Zanini, M., Jenkins, B.M. Countering the New Terrorism. Rand Corporation, Santa Monica. 1999

overall nature of the terrorist threat to national security or national objectives'. All researchers are aware that their own perspective colors what they study; objectivity is always bounded in some measure by the context the researcher works in. Lesser seems to be proposing a way of thinking about terrorism that explicitly takes one position – national security and objectives – on which to base our understanding of terrorist violence. However, a difficulty with any analysis based on assumptions like this is that other countries or cultures of course do not necessarily share those perspectives. Furthermore, by grounding analysis in the perspective of the interests of a single State or nation, limits the critical analysis so necessary for collective rational policy development faced with global rather than national crises.

However, experience suggests that the approach suggested by Lesser has gained currency and strength in the years since its publication. In particular, the current 'War on Terrorism' seems to many people to be largely based on an analysis draw on a particular sense of national interest (primarily US) even when appeal is made to aspirations that might seem of more general appeal, such as the development of democracy. References by President Bush in his speeches to America as the hope of all mankind, and drawing on biblical references to 'a light shining in the darkness that the darkness will not overcome' [17] do little other than reinforce this narrow sense of understanding the world, and paradoxically generate and sustain suspicion and opposition, in the context of culture conflict.

As noted above, contemporary analyses of terrorism increasingly tend to adopt a single dimension State perspective related to national interest. By this I mean that terrorism is frequently seen as a problem inflicted on a State by someone or something essentially outside of, or in opposition to that State even though the opposition may be a part of the citizenry; in a sense something 'other' than the State, even if a part of it. Terrorism therefore is seen as something generated by 'others', the actions of outside group or individual in opposition to the State. Characterizing the terrorist as 'evil' or 'deranged' in some sense, as so

---

17 The light shines in the darkness, and the darkness has not overcome. John, 1:5.

frequently happens, reinforces the sense of 'otherness'. Alternatively, sometimes the language of psychology is drawn on to characterize the terrorist in negative terms and again to distance him or her from normal society.

If we were trying to understand this from a psychological perspective, the logic of this is suspiciously like the process in psychology known as the 'fundamental attribution error'; whenever people are making attributions about an action, they tend to over-emphasize dispositional factors about the actor, and under-emphasize situational factors. Thus 'we' respond to circumstances. 'They' are mad or bad! However, what follows from this is that the illegitimacy of terrorism lies not in the act of violence per se, but <u>also</u> in the challenge to the interests and objectives of the State attacked <u>and</u> in the nature of the individuals committing the violence. Explanations in these terms are complex, and do not readily reduce to meaningful policy initiatives, yet solution to such ways of structuring the problem are often characterized in simple terms of 'war' or 'fight', implying defeat and victory as possible and perhaps desired outcomes.

In the heightened emotional state of the 'war on terrorism', questioning the legitimacy of conventional analyses of this kind can seem almost traitorous, and dissent can be regarded as unpatriotic. Furthermore, given this simple view it is often implicitly assumed that when the problem of terrorist violence is solved through victory, the issues associated with terrorism will also be solved, or at least become manageable. Therefore, analyses of terrorist risk, for example, tend to focus on the terrorism threats to the State as a whole, variously conceptualized as threatening the State itself, the social fabric of society, or critical economic instillations. Even when the threat relates to potential civilian causalities, the problem is conceptualized as primarily a State issue. The response to such analyses is action in some form; perhaps in terms of increased surveillance, and improved protection, and the development of response capacity. However, increasingly in the modern world, such responses are not confined to reactive protective measures, but are also pre-emptive measures (sometimes referred to as the precautionary approach). If risk can be identified, risk reduction logically implies pre-emptive action to diminish risk, in effect stopping a threat from becoming an event.

There are at least three problems with this approach. The first and obvious point is that threat and risk analysis to be effective has to be accurate. Inaccurate analysis, and consequent inappropriate pre-emptive action can add to, rather than diminish risk, (although a further problem is that single dimension analyses may not even recognize the significance of this if risk extends outside of a narrow sense of national interest). The second related problem is that risks are rarely self-contained and limited to specific foci. Risks generally occur in clusters, and can rarely be conceptualized in just single terms. Dealing with one threat may not necessarily address other collateral and dependent threats, which when viewed from a broader perspective outside of a narrow national security view may in fact be of greater significance than the original threat. The growth in willingness to engage in suicide bombings, whilst it may not have been possible to anticipate, is probably of great long-term significance as indicative of motivation and commitment, factors very relevant to our understanding of contemporary problems. The third, and perhaps most significant issue, is that by focusing on immediate threat <u>to a State</u>, there is often a failure to recognize that States in responding to terrorism may also themselves cause further terrorism by way of response.

A further weakness in the current focus on threat analysis and precautionary pre-emptive action that can be identified is that there are often implicit assumptions embedded in proposed solutions that direct responses down at times inappropriate directions:

1. Defining terrorism as a national security problem emphasizing dispositional qualities of perpetrators (as opposed to a response to circumstances), narrows analysis, and tends to imply that in principle a solution can be found, and that furthermore that solutions will lie outside of existing State structures, and relate to the qualities of the terrorist and how he or she constructs the world; the assumed 'otherness' of terrorism deflects attention from the role of the State. And implicit in this is that when the

problem is fixed the problem of terrorism will then be solved and go away;

2. Finding solutions generally implies action: and because terrorism often involves violent action, so solutions tend towards violent action solutions. But action can have illusory qualities – as Conrad says in Nostromo, "Action is consolatory. It is the enemy of thought and the friend of flattering illusions." Indeed, action not only affects the object of action, it also has a reciprocal effect on the political and psychological needs of the people undertaking action. Put simply, action might make you feel better when you are doing it, but feeling better doesn't necessarily have the desired effect on the object of the action, and in this context may not solve the problems that give rise to terrorism. The short-term consequences of responding and doing something may not be in the long term a productive response.

3. A further variant on this is the inappropriate use and dependence on technical solutions to problems. For example, complex systems of biometrics proposed for use in identity cards are unlikely to have any significant effect on terrorism – biometrics are of no value in identifying people you don't already know - yet they are attractive because it is doing something that looks complex and sophisticated.

Probably, many of these problems arise because of faulty conceptual analysis. A terrorist act is not an event, disconnected from history and context; it is a process, and understanding terrorism requires that recognition. And the very essence of a process is that it implies in some measure the recognition of a degree of reciprocity between the various elements. Put simply, action begets action, which in turn begets further action. Cycles of reciprocity can be broken, but only when the nature of relationships can be seen, understood and addressed; in pharmacological terms, the rate limiting quality needs to be identified. The nature of the forces involved in terrorism is that they are not just military or political; they involve social, economic and cultural factors as well, and a failure to address these factors on a broad front will not address, let alone resolve, the problem of terrorism.

Recent experience in Iraq and Ireland, to name but two locations, suggests that these lessons have not yet been learned. With reference to Iraq, this quotation from Stern (2003) [18] sums up the situation which many people will feel is accurate '…If bin Laden were writing a script for George Bush and Tony Blair to follow, would he not command them to attack and occupy a Muslim country in defiance of the international community and in violation of international law? And would it not be his fondest wish to see the "new crusaders" humiliate those Muslims, and themselves, in the most graphic possible way. Having those soldiers then photograph their crimes might have seemed too much to ask for.' This analysis suggests it is not necessary to attribute sophisticated powers of analysis to bin Laden to explain the persistence and significance of the war in Iraq.

4. The new challenges of terrorism

Now, great changes have taken place in the terrorism concepts and tactics. The nature of terrorism seems to be different now from 10 or 20 years ago. 9/11 may be seen in the US as a watershed, but there are good grounds for suggesting that these changes predate 9/11, and related more to the changing nature of global politics after the demise of the Soviet Union, and the increasing globalization of economic and political activities.

How can we characterize this change in terrorism? Raufer (2003) [19] describes the features of the new terrorism. According to Raufer analysis the following six broad qualities might characterize the new terrorist threat. Not all terrorism necessarily shares all these qualities and of course old terrorist conflicts remain; but taken together they do seem to capture the qualities of difference new terrorism implications:

---

18 Stern, J. Fearing Evil. Social Research, 2003, 71, 1111-1126.
19 Raufer, Xavier. Al Qaeda: A Different Diagnosis. Studies in Conflict and Terrorism, 2003, 26, 391-398.

- Lack of specific territorial base, and/ or location in inaccessible areas (geographically and socially)

The new terrorism tends to be either physically or socially located in areas that are difficult to access. The most obvious example is physical inaccessibility, which may result when despite modern transport, the geography of terrorist location reduces and limits access (through geographical isolation as in Afghanistan for example, or through the inaccessibility in the vast unplanned urban areas that characterize the major cities of many developing countries). Social inaccessibility, in parallel with geographical inaccessibility, refers to the social 'grey areas' and the growing underclass of modern urban cities, where social poverty and exclusion as much as economic poverty and exclusion creates a fertile environment for dissent. Ironically, as Castells notes, exclusion from the new technologies might also fall within this category of social exclusion (Castells 2000 [20]).

- Absence of third party state control through sponsorship

A feature of much of the terrorism of the 1980's and 90's was its surrogate quality. Terrorist groups had sometimes explicit, but more often covert relationships with governments, who supported their activities, and gave them direction. Of course state support for terrorism remains in the modern world, but its significance seems to be reduced, and in particular terrorist organizations seem to show reduced dependence on a single source of funding. We should note that old terrorist groups, such as the Provisional IRA, never had the close ties to governments as Middle Eastern groups did, and had a much more populist quality to fund raising.

- Absence of structured command hierarchy and management system.

---

20 Castells, M. The Information Age. Economy, Society and Culture. Vols. 1-3. Blackwell, Oxford. 2000

Perhaps the greatest difference between the contemporary terrorist world and the past is the changed nature of terrorist organizations. Direction in the past came from hierarchically structured organizations, which despite cell structures, maintained control over action and planning. Through such hierarchical structures, sponsoring States could of course exercise control. In the contemporary world, terrorist organizations seem to have the following characteristics:

o   Dispersed flat cellular structure.
o   Decisions result from informal hierarchy based on trust.

This is not to suggest that hierarchical control no longer exists, but rather that in operation it is much more dispersed, and local activists are less tightly tied to the center – indeed there may not be a center in any conventional management sense. Contemporary terrorist organizations do not need a home base from which to operate from. They have adopted a globalized agenda, and are moving towards the creation of what in Information Technology terms is a form of virtual organization.

Perhaps the most significant quality that enables this structure to be sustained is the use of low tech and personal trust communication. Communication between groups and individuals seems to have reverted to forms of communication dependent on personal contact, and knowledge and trust of individuals. This is not a phenomenon unique to contemporary terrorism; many groups and organizations who place a premium on confidentiality and certainty have in the past, and continue, to use such communication structures for secure communication. Hasidic diamond traders in New York and Antwerp, businesses in industrial areas in Northern Italy and overseas Chinese entrepreneurs, for example, use similar techniques dependent on personal contact, passage of written communication and reliance on word of mouth in negotiating business deals. Such communication is, however, inconvenient for the security services, and of course simply bi-passes the structures of interception and surveillance. As a result, it of course exposes the weakness of dependence on high tech surveillance for intelligence gathering.

- Hybrid ideological character - partly "political" or religious-fanatic, partly criminal

Along with changes in the organizational structure of terrorist groups have come changes in the nature of their membership. These changes can be characterized as:

o   highly motivated membership;
o   significance of local context;
o   range of attacks, range of targets.

They also have the ability to rapidly mutate or change direction, to exploit low frequency high impact action and show a broad target range. This suggests a much more pragmatic approach to target selection where symbolic targets and practical targets might be equally likely to be addressed.

In this context, we can identify two major differences between the contemporary terrorist group and its past ancestors. The first is the capacity and willingness to deploy and use enormous killing potential, compared with Cold-War symbolic terrorism. The ideological agonizing that characterized the Baadermeinhof Group, for example, in its choice of tactics seems totally absent now, replaced by a much more pragmatic and ruthless form of terrorism, where the risk of civilian casualties seems to have no moral role in decisions about targets and casualties. The second major difference is the nature of the ideological context to contemporary terrorism. The strength of contemporary ideological commitment can be seen in the willingness of young people to present themselves as suicide bombers (as noted earlier I would suggest this is a measure of commitment rather than psychopathy). State funding of terrorism seems to have been replaced by funding derived from other, often criminal, activity; but whilst many commentators predicted the growing absorption of terrorist groups into criminal activity with the demise of communism and the bi-polar conflict, the ideological and religious context to contemporary terrorist organization seems to be able to sustain a terrorist agenda as well as engage in criminal fund raising.

However, it is important to note that this is not new – the Provisional IRA, as a historical example, has always engaged in criminal fund raising. What is new is the use of such tactics by terrorist groups that address trans-national agendas.

A brief comparison of an old (Provisional Irish Republican Army) and new (Al Qaeda) types of terrorist groups will perhaps help develop the discussion. There are several paramilitary groups that either claim or have claimed the title Irish Republican Army (IRA). The basic central objective of all of these groups is to seek to create a unitary Irish state with no constitutional ties to the United Kingdom.

PIRA explicitly adopts the language of the military to describe its structures, reflecting of course it's supposed origins as the 'legitimate' army of the Irish Republic, as well as being a pragmatic response to circumstances. Military titles are used to describe functions (brigadiers, officers commanding), and the structure, whilst at ground level is expressed in cells, has a clear and explicit hierarchical character – terms such as Units and Brigades are used which have a geographical base. An 'Army' Council controls and authorizes activity. Uniforms, parades, marching – all the trappings of a military organization are deployed when necessary to give the impression of legitimacy as an army for both political and historical reasons.

If we take Al Qaeda as an example of new terrorism, we can immediately see differences. Al Qaeda does not explicitly adopt the trappings of military organizations, and does not seem to see the need to make these claims for political legitimacy. Its members may wear what look like uniforms (in terms of commonality of dress) but they are not the uniforms of armies. Whilst the West seeks to characterize Al Qaeda as an organization with a clear hierarchy (controlled by bin Laden) the reality is that it is simply not that kind of organization. It is dispersed, decentralized, and capable of functioning in the absence of explicit leadership. Perhaps most important of all, Al Qaeda does not draw from a single ethnic or national base. Its dispersed membership seems to be almost global in character, reflecting the spread of Islam. And because it has global affiliations (if not membership) so its operations can be mounted almost anywhere. Its targets seem to be equally diffuse, and whilst the war in Iraq has provided a focus, its ideological character is not grounded in the Iraqi experience, or any other particular national experience: its agenda transcends the nation state.

This, more than anything, perhaps gives the key to understanding the difference between the national and regional terrorist structures we are used to from the cold war days, and the contemporary terrorist structures. In cultural terms the terrorist groups of the late twentieth century were familiar to Western audiences. They could be understood from a Western cultural perspective, and their actions although reprehensible, were understandable from the Western historical and social context. Modern terrorism in contrast is not familiar to the Western world-view. Concepts like 'Jihad' are not familiar to Western audiences, and the assumptions of Islam are not necessarily at all obvious to non-Muslims. Structures, agendas and the logic of action that draws on these cultural roots do not easily fit into Western thinking. Yet paradoxically, as noted earlier, instead of taking a broad cultural perspective to understanding this new terrorism, we have moved towards an increasingly ethnocentric approach to understanding terrorism.

What we are experiencing may not be so much as a 'Clash of Civilizations' but more a failure to understand cultural and associated ideological assumptions, and at its most benign this failure results in efforts to impose the values of one culture and tradition on another, perhaps inadvertently, perhaps deliberately. Qutb's exhortation to Islam that 'We need a unified ideology to confront life and its problems, an ideology that will solidify our strength against our foreign and domestic enemies' perhaps should be taken much more seriously by the West than hitherto in the light of current experience. In this may lie the key to understanding the relevance of the war in Iraq to the growth of terrorism, and similarly the irrelevance of the war to the defeat of contemporary terrorism.

5. Globalization and terrorism

How can we understand the power of modern terrorism? One answer to this may lie in the ideological and religious bases of organizations like Al Qaeda, which have through that ideological background broken free of their regional base. I see no evidence of a sophisticated ideology emerging from the particular writings or pronouncements of Al Qaeda members, and particularly from bin Laden, but in a sense this does not matter. Al Qaeda can draw on the rich ideological groundwork laid by Qutb, Turrabi and others, who has revived the extensive works of the early Muslim scholars, such as Ibn Taymiya, Ibn Al Qayym, Ibn Katheer and others, in their critique of both contemporary Muslims and their relationship with the West. However, we might also identify other factor that may reflect upon this complex problem.

The role of the media is one such important factor. In a regional sense, there seems to have been a degree of public desensitization to violence. Irish terrorism, for example, seems not to be so effective in its actions since the 1998 Manchester bombing. I suspect the constant playing and replaying of the agony of 9/11 on a global scale generates complex and inconsistent effects in many societies, with not always positive consequences on views about the US. And the growing tendency to not offer attribution to attacks adds to a sense of complexity, uncertainty and fear that the media often reflects and exaggerates. In a specific sense the role of the media in the war in Iraq remains to be fully understood, but is clearly critical. The globalization of the media, in terms of coverage and scale, is central to the shaping of our understanding of events; but what is perhaps surprising is that despite the trend towards monopoly in the Western news media, there remains substantial independence in carrying alternative views and accounts. The Internet and the ease of transmission of information has probably played an important part in this.

Other factors such as availability of weapons, the relative financial independence from State sponsorship of contemporary terrorism (as noted earlier) and the capacity to be creative and innovative (perhaps because of the lack of hierarchical structure) are also clearly relevant, but a further single factor is the attitude to risk and risk management. Perhaps because of the shock to the US Government of 9/11, and the clear failings in the security systems of the US that allowed it to happen, the generalized perception of risk seems to have increased. Sometimes this seem to be in the absence of objective supportive evidence, perhaps the result of a fear of making a mistake; at other times there seems to be evidence that political factors have led to the use of heightened risk for political ends. A factor facilitating this is a confusion of potential risk and real risk, and nowhere has this been more evident than with respect to terrorism and the new technologies. Potential risks, however distant and unlikely are often included in risk analyses without discount or discrimination. For example, there have been no known examples of cyber-terrorism (in the sense that we might understand other forms of terrorism), yet news media frequently carry stories highlighting terrorist potential risk in commercial and other computer systems. There clearly are high risk activities being conducted on the Internet involving for example viruses and commercial fraud – but there is little or no evidence of any involvement of terrorists in these activities.

For example, in 1999 there were persistent news reports that the course of a newly launched Skynet satellite, a part of the UK military communications systems, had been changed by hackers. There is no evidence that this in fact happened, but there are some grounds for thinking that such an aspiration might have formed the basis of a blackmail attempt – a dramatic story certainly, but lacking terrorist substance and probably belonging to a more mundane criminal context. More recently, reports have emerged of claims that Al Qaida has the capacity to engage in cyber-terrorism, based largely on the content of seized computers. When these reports are looked at in detail, however, it turns out that the supposed cyber-terrorism capacity amounts to the presence of software on computers that may indeed facilitate hacking, but which would be shared by literally tens of thousands of children and students who use the Internet recreationally. Whilst the potential for hacking may be present, the reality seems to be lacking.

Furthermore, there is persistent confusion between the use of the new technologies for communication, the use of the Internet for propaganda and news dissemination and the use of active hacking into sensitive targets to effect some terrorist objective. There is no evidence of the latter ever having been done by a terrorist group. There is certainly evidence of the use of the Internet for communication, but in this the terrorist is sharing a capacity used by millions upon millions of people. Such communication is of course fundamentally insecure, a point not lost on the new terrorist. There is also evidence of Internet sites and other IT based media being changed or tampered with for political objectives. For example, Falun Gong, the Chinese religious organization, apparently took over Chinese satellite TV broadcasts on 2002. According to Sino Satellite Communications, two of its Sinosat-1 transponders were hijacked in late June 2002, interrupting TV transmissions of state broadcaster CCTV's nine TV channels to rural villages, during which time "Falun Gong propaganda materials" were broadcast. This reportedly also happened on two earlier occasions. It seems likely, however, that this substitution of TV material originated in ground station feeds through the actions of employees, rather than a hacking into the satellite communication system as such.

Governments are sensitive to the propaganda value of the expression through the Internet of civil dissent of this kind. The recent Open Net initiative study on censorship identified Iran, Saudi Arabia and China (amongst others) as countries attempting to limit Internet access not only to pornographic and similar sites of moral or religious concern, but also to web material of a political nature. But making available such material does not amount to example of cyber terrorism (although of course it might be argued that limiting access does).

6. Future of terrorism:

It is a dangerous thing to try to predict the future. The future has a habit of playing tricks on us and in its failure to respect what we with our short term limited vision might regard as absolute truths, it reveals the transitory and limited nature of our assumptions. So the point from which I will seek to draw my vision of the future will in time also be revealed as incomplete and flawed. Looking to the future is hard enough. But to understand terrorism I believe we have also to try to understand the broader problem of what influences behaviour, terrorist or otherwise, as a reflection of what are essentially behavioral processes. And such processes are notoriously difficult to conceptualize and understand. It is also inappropriate to talk in specific terms about the future of terrorism in a continent as diverse as Europe. Given all of this, all I can hope to do in indicate what from my perspective are some general principles that might make us better able to understand future terrorist conflict, and to try to illustrate these from within a specific context. In any discussion of political terrorism undertaken over the past twenty years (and I am largely confining my discussion to political terrorism), I suspect there would have been broad agreement over both what political terrorism was, and how we might understand its origins. In the main, the term has been used to refer to violence which in some way tries to influence the political agenda of a state, frequently seeking to destabilize, overthrow or radically change it. Predominantly, but not exclusively, we have become used to characterizing political terrorism in terms of left-right dimensions or considering them as outlaws or corruptors.

There are other issues related to the future of terrorism that must be referred to. We know that the availability of weapons and munitions are central factors in determining terrorist activity. The terrorist may be a rational actor, but the rate limiting factor in the process of terrorist development is at one level availability of ammunitions and explosives. More alarming are the reports of the availability of high tech weapons, and in particular weapons with either a nuclear or biological potential. That such weapons should fall into the hands of a terrorist or organization has been a continuing fear for many years, and probability of this happening seems to have increased somewhat.

Terrorism is not caused by any single factor; it is a complex state, and the individual involved in terrorism has been subjected to a wide array of influences related to family, tribe, community settings and identity. Nor is the terrorism mad. We tend to think that because their tactics are so barbaric, they must be barbaric, how else we can understand them. But if they were not mad, and if they were not suffering from some personality or other disorder, we are left with the uncomfortable fact that the terrorist is in many ways rather like us. They can be distinguished from us because of what they do, but I don't believe there is any evidence to suggest that they differ in any psychological dimensions from none terrorists. We must also never forget that terrorism exists within society and their actions represent community issues that they are unable to spell out verbally.

In a work published a few years ago, Taylor tried to develop a way of thinking about the causes of terrorism that could draw in a general way upon both psychological and social process. He suggested that we could think of terrorism as the product of three major forces that found expression at a social, political and psychological level. When these factors become present, we see political dissent turning towards violence. Whatever the new world offers, it is sure that these fundamental qualities of people will remain, and we will continue to witness terrorism as a factor in the conflicts.

There is no doubt at all that as a tool within broader conflicts, terrorism will continue to flourish and develop. But rather than seeing terrorism as the instrument of ideological struggle, we will see the growth of terrorism related to civilizations as an element in a broader concept of warfare. Rise in terrorism related to inter-civilization disputes will remain, sometimes because of more straight forward disputes over power or money, and sometimes because of strongly held ideology or moral views. All of these various facets of terrorism will happen because terrorism is and remains an attractive tool for disaffected groups and groupings to exercise a disproportionate influence.

All is not gloom and despair. New forms of terrorism will adapt and change to circumstances, but it does not necessarily follow that the world cannot respond. We too, as the unwilling victims and spectators of terrorism must also adapt and change. However, responses will need to be much more sophisticated that those currently deployed, and in particular, the emphasis on military responses as a core policy support will have to be re-assessed. I believe policy needs to focus on two levels:

o addressing the immediate context to terrorism and its management;
o addressing the causes and sustaining features of social dysfunction that support the emergence of terrorism.

In addressing the immediate context to terrorism, military responses may play a part, but the core effort needs to be through civil society structures drawing on local and regional contexts. All too often military responses impede the emergence of civil structures, and experience suggests that the logic of the military creating the conditions for civil society to develop is flawed. However, few resources have been put into understanding the role of civil society in the management of terrorism, and it seems to me that this needs much greater investment to explore models, processes and techniques to gain maximum effect. Evidence based policy development in this area needs to be encouraged and sustained. It is only through civil society structures that the cultural and social context that supports terrorism can be addressed. Regardless of any ideological context, in simple practical terms this seems a reasonable way forward.

An important element of any civil society response will be to use the new technologies to support and develop initiatives. When facing a decentralized terrorist system, the power of many can combat decentralized foes:

o　As we have noted contemporary terrorist networks are highly decentralized and distributed. A centralized effort by itself cannot effectively fight this kind of terrorism

o　Terrorism is everyone's issue and the Internet connects everyone. A connected citizenry is the best defense against terrorist propaganda

o　As we saw in the aftermath of the March 11 bombing in Spain, the response was spontaneous and rapid because the citizens were able to use the Internet to organize themselves.

o　As we are seeing in the distributed world of weblogs and other kinds of citizen media, truth emerges best in open conversation among people with divergent views. But the corollary of that is that truth can sometimes be challenging and uncomfortable.

Indeed, these processes may challenge the policy assumptions adopted by some States; but through them I believe we can also address the second policy focus of addressing the causes and sustaining features of social dysfunction that support the emergence of terrorism. The Internet is not the panacea for all the ills of society, but the strength of resistance to it from States that fear openness is a measure of the potential they see in it for generating change. We may never eliminate terrorism, but we can strive to reduce and contain it. But to achieve that end there will need to be substantial changes in the nature of governance in many States towards openness and a functioning civil society.

THREE

AL-QAEDA PATTERN OF JIHAD

1. What is Al-Qaeda

Anyone who attempts to study or examine the links between contemporary terrorism and Islamic Jihad, cannot ignore Al-Qaeda, because, there is now a general consensus in the western media and among the great majority of the public, that Al-Qaeda is behind terroristic activities targeting the western nations. Although by such consensus, Al-Qaeda might be given more than its real volume. Moreover, there is still a widespread disagreement over what Al-Qeada is. It is remarkable that, after more than two decades has passed since Al-Qaeda establishment, and despite of its involvement in open confrontations with International super powers, Al-Qaeda remains as a poorly understood phenomenon among the western scholars. What is Al-Qaeda? Is it —as the questions raised by Raufer- a clearinghouse, an extremist Islamist group, a global network, an entity, an organization, a system, a secret international brotherhood, a powerful Islamic force or a dispersed and amorphous terrorist foe? Does it have cells and operative members; does it function like a cult or like an enterprise? [21]

---

21 Xavier Raufer, "Al-Qeada: A Different Diagnosis" Studies in conflict & terrorism, 26:391-398,2003

During the 1st decade of this century, no individual, organization or human activity was focused by western writers and traced by western experts and analysts more than the term Al-Qaeda. Nevertheless, we are still far away from understanding what does the term Al-Qaeda mean in the context of the contemporary Islamic movements or terrorism. It took many pages and innumerable books and articles in western literature to explain the term Al-Qaeda, and to find its roots in Arabic language as well as in history. On the contrary, in the Arab world and among Muslim scholars, the term Al-Qaeda has never been a focus of researchers or emphasis of the analysts. That was, in fact, a fruitful indication for the western writers, who has placed all their efforts on a single leaf of one tree in a forest. A single leaf (like Al –Qaeda) which grows normally and drops shortly while the trees and the forest remain deeply rooted.

The term Al-Qaeda itself is not critical as thought by several western writers.[22] Al-Qaeda is and Arabic word, simply meaning a base or foundation. The term Al-Qaeda was used in the context of contemporary Islamic movement, for the first time in 1987 by Abduallah Azzam, the leader of Arab-Afghan mujahidin who fought against the Soviets in Afghanistan. Azzam has referred in his writings and speeches to the terms "Talliat" which means the vanguard and "Al-Qaeda Alsulba"", meaning strong foundation or base. Azzam envisaged his group of mujahidin as the "Talliat Al-Qaeda Al-sulba or the vanguard of the strong foundation for the new Islamic society. Al-sulba

According to the western writer's evidence concluded mainly from CIA reports and FBI investigations, Al-Qaeda emerged as coherent and structured group of freedom fighters began its activities in Pakistan and Afghanistan by late 1980 under Abullah Azzam, Usama Bin Laden and several Arab militants from Egypt, Saudi Arabia, Algeria and Kuwait.

According to (165) pages of very poor handwritten reports maintained by Internal Security Department of the Sudanese government during (1987-1990), a large group of Arab-Afghan Mujahidin began to move to

---

22 Jason Burke, Al-Qaeda – The true story of Radical Islam. London: penguin Books,2003

Khartoum, the capital of Sudan, which was politically well controlled by the Islamic party known as National Islamic front, under the leadership of Hassen Al-Turabi. The security reports have indicated that those Mujahidin were well organized, so friendly and wealthy enough to rent houses in the most elegant parts of the city such as Riyadh and Manshiya. They used to refer to those houses as "bayt Al Qaeda" however the term never draws the attention at that time. Therefore, it is obvious that Sudan and the Sudanese Islamists were popular destination of Arab-Afghan at that time. It was in the mind of the Egyptian Islamic Jihad leader Ayman Al-Zawahiri to consider Sudan as a second choice to locate the Mujahidin, primarily to enhance the political activities of his organization in the neighboring Egypt. Fortunately, as Al-Zawahiri has expected, the Islamic regime took power in Khartoum in 1989, making it more encouraging to move Al-Qaeda project from Afghanistan to Sudan. Although, the Arab Afghan began flowing into the Sudanese capital since 1987, their political and religious plans were not known to the Sudanese authorities, till 1990.

In 1991, Bin Laden who was under house arrest in Jeddah, the second major city of the Saudi Arabia, found himself helpless in front of the difficulties which were facing his plans to mobilize the Muslim world beginning from the Arab peninsula. There, he thought in following the "Sunna" by imitating the prophet Mohammed's migration from Mecca to Madeena in the Sixth century. Bin Laden could successfully fly from Jeddah to Pakistan's city of Peshawar, and within two or three months, he left Peshawar to Khartoum. Although Al-Jazeera television, Al-Quds Al-Arabia reports and many other intelligence data indicated that Bin Laden's arrival to Sudan was in 1992, however, according the Sudanese security reports, he has arrived in Khartoum on October 1991.

During his stay in Sudan, Bin Laden and his fellow Arab Afghan has found a favorable political and social environment to thoroughly discuss the future activities and formulate strategies and develop alternative plans. The period between 1992 and 1996 was the most fruitful years for Al-Qaeda leaders. Following introduction of Sharia in Sudan in 1991, the country was wide-opened for the Muslim scholars and Islamic movement leaders from all over the world who found their way to Al

Qaeda leaders and exchange expertise. The new Islamic government under the patronage of Hassen Al-Turabi, who was known as the power behind the throne has organized a series of international conferences inviting Islamic scholars, Islamic militant activists and veterans of the Afghanistan Mujahidin to discuss issues related Islam and politics in the Arab and Islamic countries. Such environment made it possible for Bin-laden to meet with innumerable Muslim activists and develop his own connections and enhance what later became Al-Qaeda network throughout the world.

Al-Turabi and his allies in the Islamic government of General Omer Hassen Al Bashsir were looking at Bin Laden as a businessman who is going to support the new Islamic state by funding development projects, however, Bin Laden was actually devoted to setting up his own Islamic Agenda. Hassen Al-Turabi, one of the leading figures of contemporary Islamic movements was also very ambitious politician with his own Islamic Agenda. With his Salafist background and traditional Quranic education, a degree in law from the University of Khartoum, a master's from the University of London and a doctorate from the Sorbonne, had developed his Islamic party since 1960, based on Hassen Al-Banna's Muslim brotherhood which was founded in 1944. However, his real goal was not limited to Al-Banna teaching, he was fighting to develop his own school of a global politic Islam.

By taking the power and introducing sharia in Sudan, Hassen Al-Turabi, decided to devote himself to global Islamic activities. In 1991, Al-Turabi has established a regional umbrella for political Islamist organization, known as popular Arab Islamic conference (PAIC), with its head office in Khartoum, and with the aim of confronting America and its allies in the region. Turabi becoming the secretary general of (PAIC), has also contributed in opening the Sudan for all Arabs including Usama Bin Laden and the Arab Afghan. In the light of the open deliberations of international conferences and meetings sponsored by the Sudanese government, it was obvious that Al-Turabi and Bin laden were with different objectives and controversial strategies. Although, both leaders were Wahhabi-Salafist oriented, Al-Turabi was politician rather than religious leader, while Bin-Laden was religious leader rather than a politician. Consequently, disputes between the two leaders began to emerge in 1994. Thus while Al-Turabi was planning to go ahead in changing the governments in the Arab and Islamic countries by political and peaceful means including peaceful military coups, Bin Laden and his followers, benefiting the free religious debates sponsored by Al_Turabi and the Sudanese government, were completely engaged in organizing their networks and enhancing a broad movement of sympathizers and militants at national, regional and international levels.

In the open conferences and debates, Bin Laden and his Arab Afghan used to focus on over throwing Al-Saud family and their American allies out of the Arab peninsula, to establish the Islamic state of Al-Hijaz instead of the Kingdom of Saudi Arabia. However, behind the closed doors, Al-Turabi used to advocate existence of Al Saud family and their kingdom as the most favorable environment where new Islamists are grown and Islamic teachings are maintained.

The hard-Core of Al-Qaeda leadership including Ayman Al-Zawahiri, Mohammed Al-Zawahiri, Tariq al_fadhli, Mohammed Odeh, Mohammed Atef, Khalid Shaikh, Ramzi Yousef and Mohammed Rashid Al-Owhali was strengthened. At this moment Bin Laden outlined his message which was entitled declaration of war against Americans, which was issued later in 23rd of August 1996. The document which was considered as the guidelines of Al-Qaeda protocol has stated the following objectives:

o   Addressing Muslims all over the world and in the Arab peninsula specifically.

o   Declaration of war against the Americans occupying the land of the holy places (Kingdom of Saudi Arabia) and the ruling family of Al-Saud.

o   Focusing the miserable political, socio-economic situation and injustice of the rulers, due to straying from the correct Islamic way.

o   Looking at the family of Al-Saud as hypocrites and unbelievers who must be resisted.

o   Justification of Jihad against occupiers of the Arab peninsula as a defensive war and a duty of every individual Muslim.

o   Extending Jihad beyond Arab peninsula to end repression of the Islamic world by the crusader and Zionists and their alliances.

o   Emphasizing the role of the youth of Saudi Arabia, calling them to vanguard.

o   Giving priority for attacking the Crusader-Zionist alliance, emphasizing USA and other representatives of global disbelievers (kufar), who are the greater enemies, before attacking the rulers of the Middle East, who are the smaller enemies.

Thus Al-Qaeda came to exist within a wide open network with many unorganized groups and leaders empowered by great number of supporters and sympathizers, but unified – in general under the concept outlined by Usama Bin Laden.

Today, Al-Qaeda of Bin Laden and Al Zawahri has lost more than 75% of its powers and organizational influence. However, the theories, protocols military strategies and operations adopted and conducted by Al-Qaeda during the last two decades are now undertaken by new generations and sponsored by more sophisticated clandestine groups in many parts of the world. There is evidence that Al-Qaeda protocols are being considered even by non-Islamic clandestine groups suffering from socio-economic injustice. Therefore, defeating deeply rooted ideological organizations may not be deemed victory, unless their protocols, allegations and attractive slogans are defeated or solved.

2. Suicide terrorism

Suicide terrorism is one of the most prominent features of contemporary terrorism, and one of the most difficult to understand. Suicide missions have occurred in many countries and within deferent cultures. To Understand the suicide terrorism one ought to take into account a great variety of circumstances and motives and should not focus on one specific group or religion. [23]

Those who are willing to sacrifice their own life must be instigated by a great and noble cause according to individuals believe and inner concern. However, in the light of the objectives of this study we have to examine whether suicide terrorism is a pattern of Jihad or not. Also we have to understand how and by what means individuals are psychologically reformed to become successful suicide performers.

According to the most authenticated sources of Islam, suicide is forbidden. The majority of various religious dignitaries who have totally opposed and condemned all patterns of suicide bombings. Other religious scholars have justified suicide bombing as shahada (martyrdom), and a third group has taken a middle way position.[24] Such hesitant and unclear explanations for one of the most contemporary dilemmas of global concern was not favorable element for Muslim scholars.

Sheikh Muhammad Tantawi, head of Al Azhar, gave two opinions in this context. On one occasion, he considered that all Israelis, including men, women and children – were forces of occupation and legitimate targets of suicide bombers. On another occasion he said that no Muslim should blow himself up in the midst of children and women, but only among aggressors and soldiers. Yusuf Al Qaradawi, has declared that suicide terrorism is the heights form of Jihad. Sheikh Sabri, the Mufti of Jerusalem considered suicide bombing as heroic actions of obeying a religious duty, Therefore, the available evidence is in favor of those who justify suicide bombing as Jihad and consider suicide bombers as martyrdom,

* *What is suicide terrorism?*

Over the past two or three decades' suicide terrorism has become a distinctive phenomenon, related mostly to religious-oriented terrorist organizations. Suicide terrorism is defined as 'a politically motivated

---

23 Walter Liqueur, No End to War: Terrorism in the Twenty- Firs century. New York: continuum,2004, P.71

24 Names, nationalities of responding scholars with held on their request

violent attack perpetrated by a self-aware individual or individuals who actively and purposely causes his own death. Different forms and patterns of suicide attacks been known in the history of human conflicts; however, contemporary suicide terrorism started in Lebanon in 1983, by a group of Muslims known by the name of Hezbollah. This group organized the first suicide attack on American embassy in Beirut, followed by an attack on the U.S. Marines headquarters, in the same year.

Terroristic suicide attack can result in many casualties and extensive damage. It is most preferred by helpless groups and individuals who are motivated by self-sacrifice for the sake of their rights and objectives. Furthermore, suicide attacks do not require escape plans or fear of being arrested, in addition to the religious or political benefits the perpetrator and his family earn (according to his belief).

Suicide operations, are known in Islam as a fighting by operation organized groups to cause losses among the army of the enemy and cause economical and psychological damage by clandestine activities, performed by selected units of the army according to the authorization of the Immam[25].

The Chechen rebels, the Kurdistan workers' party and the Sri Lankan Liberation Tigers of Tamil Elma are known to be amongst the most brutal organizations utilizing suicide terrorism. However, for the purpose of this study attention is drawn to the following groups:

- The Islamic resistance movement known by Hamas, "harakat el-Mukawama el Islamiya".
- Palistinian Islamic Jihad.
- Egyptian Gama'a el -Islamiya.
- Egyptian Islamic Jihad.
- Al Qaida.

---

25 أحمد شلبي، الجهاد في التفكير الإسلامي، القاهرة، مكتبة التهضة،1968.

Suicide attacks are attractive and fruitful by the above-mentioned groups who regard them as a kind of religious worship and a divine command or Jihad, as discussed earlier.

3. The new generations of Al-Qaeda

Fouad Hussain, a Jordanian journalist wrote a book outlining reliable facts on the second generation of Al-Qaeda, based on data collected from many close members of Islamic organizations. In his book titled –Al Z arqawi : Al Jeel Al Thani Li – Al-Qaeda, Fouad has explained the strategy of Al- Qaeda and Jihad organization in Iraq up to the year 2020.According to Fouad, Al- Qaeda strategy consists of seven stages, extended through two decades, in a chronological order starting from September,11, 2001 as follows:

- The stage of awakens which started by the preparation of September 11, operation.
- The stage of opening the eyes
- The stage of renaissance, which emphasizes the area of Al-Sham.
- The stage of total recovery
- The stage of declaring Islamic state, which starts in 2013.
- The stage of confrontation,2013
- The stage of the final victory, when Islam will be victorious

Within this strategy, Al-Zarqawi and his organization of Bilad Al-Rafidain were sent to operate in Iraq. But, who is Al-Zarqawi,and how he could stand as a power in front of the super powers of the world.

- ***Who is Al Zarqawi***

Ahmed Fadel Al-Nazal Al-khalaylah, known as Abu Musab Al-Zarqawi was born in the Jordanian city of Al-Zarqa, October 20, 1966, in a poor family belonging to Bin – Hassan tribe that is one of the major Jordanian clans. He has dropped out of the formal education at the second year of the secondary school. He went to look for religious education in the neighboring Abdullah Bin Abbas Mosque, in Zarqa, where he developed friendship with different Islamic groups. At that time the only available Jihad filed for Zarqawi was fighting communists in Afghanistan. Following a lecture on Jihad made by Abel Rasoul Seyaf in Jordan, Zarqawi decided to travel to Afghanistan in late 1980s.

Zarqawi has obtained his military training and spiritual orientation at the battle field against soviet armies. Zarqawi fought beside Jelal Al-Deen Haggna and Qalb Al-Deen Hikmetyar. He participates in defeating the Russian in khast city in 1991. Zarqawi was influenced by the senior Jordanian Muslim-brother's leader Abdullah Azzam and Issam Al-Bargawi whom he met at Peshawar in 1989.

Following the withdrawal of the Soviets from Afghanistan, Zarqawi, as many Arab Afghans, decided to go back to Jordan where he attempted to cooperate with Abu Mohammed Al-Maqdisi to spread their concept of Jihad and enroll the youth Muslims for Jihad operations in Israel. However, he was arrested in1992 by the Jordanian security and sentenced with seven years of imprisonment. In 1996, during serving his imprisonment term, Zarqawi improved his religious education and gained the leadership of his colloquies. Zarqawi started his actual organizational career by establishing his own group in 1993, in cooperation with Abu Al-Muntasir Bi Allah, under the name of "Tanzim Al-Tawheed" unification organization, which was latter re-named as "Bayat Al-Immam".

In1999, Al-Zrqawi went back to Afghanistan where he met Bin laden, and became his rival due to minor differences. He established his own camp in Herat until 11, September 2001 and the American invasion of Iraq. Zarqawi established his network depending mainly on Al-Sham people and has adopted a model Islamic society through interrelation marriages among his group members. Zarqawi who was believed to be one-time rival, but now high-ranking member of Osama bin Laden's al-Qaeda militant network, and since October 2004 refers to his own organization (Jema'at Al-Tawhid – Unification and Holy War Group, an insurgent network operating in Iraq) as "Al-Qaeda in Iraq". On October 21, 2004, Zarqawi officially announced his allegiance to Al-Qaeda; on December 27, 2004, Al-Jazeera broadcast an audio-cast of bin laden calling Zarqawi "the prince of Al-Qaeda in Iraq" and asked all our organization brethren to listen to him and obey him in his good deeds".

After September, 11 attacks, Zarqawi again travelled to Afghanistan and was reportedly wounded in a U.S. bombardment. He moved to Iraq to organize Al-Tawhid, his former militant organization. Zarqawi then settled in the Kurdish-controlled region of northern Iraq. Where he joined the Islamist Ansar al-Islam group that fought against Kurdish-nationalist forces in the region. He reportedly become a leader in the group, although his leadership role has not been stablished There are rumors that Zarqawi is dead because no sightings of him have been confirmed since 2001. In one report, the conservative British Newspaper Daily Telegraph described as myth the claim that Zarqawi was the head of the "terrorist network" in Iraq. According to a U.S. military intelligence source, the Zarqawi myth resulted from faulty intelligence obtained by the payment of substantial sums of money to unreliable and dishonest sources. The faulty intelligence was accepted, however, because it suited US government political goals, according to an unnamed intelligence officer.

In March 2004, an insurgent group in Iraq issued a statement saying that Zarqawi had been killed in 2002. The statement said that he was unable to escape the missile attack because of his prosthetic leg. His followers claimed he was killed in a US bombing raid in the north of Iraq. The claim that Zarqawi had been killed in northern Iraq "at the beginning of the war", and that subsequent use of his name was a useful myth, was repeated in September 2005 by Sheikh Jawad Al-Khalessi, a Shiite imam.

On 24 May 2005 it was reported on an Islamic website that a deputy would take command of Al-Qaeda while Abu Musab al-Zarqawi recovered from injuries sustained in an attack. Later that week the Iraqi government confirmed that Zarqawi had been wounded by U.S. forces, although the battalion did not realize it at the time. The extent of his injuries is not known, although some radical Islamic websites called for prayers for his health. There are reports that a local hospital treated a man, suspected to be Zarqawi, with severe injuries. He was also said to have subsequently left Iraq for a neighboring country, accompanied by two physicians. However, later that week the radical Islamic website retracted its report about his injuries and claimed that he was in fine health and was running the Jihad operation.

In a September 16, 2005 article published by Le Monde, Sheikh Jawad Al-Kalesi claimed that al-Zarqawi was killed in the Kurdish northern region of Iraq at the beginning of the US-led war on the country as he was meeting with members of the Ansar al-Islam group affiliated to al-Qaida. Al-Kalesi also claimed "His family in Jordan even held a ceremony after his death." He also claimed that "Zarqawi has been used as a ploy by the United States, as an excuse to continue the occupation. saying that it was a pretext so they don't leave Iraq."

However, whether Zarqawi is dead or alive, Zarqawi phenomenon as the second generation of Al-Qaeda network is visible. It seems to be more powerful, more aggressive and going in line the strategy of Al-Qaeda. Therefore, the declared war against terrorism is not working.

4. Assessment of Al-Qaeda Jihad

Now, more than twenty years has passed since waging war by the super powers against terrorism, namely Al-Qaeda which no more seems to know for sure, what it is and where its location. Many innocent people have lost their life, property and freedom in the war against terrorism. Now, people are jeopardized in many parts of the world due to war against terrorism from one side and terrorism from the other, it is the real state of terror. Security measures based on poor intelligence taken in many countries is terrifying, the directives and the cautionary declarations issued from time to time are terrifying, and the most unoptimistic sigh is the statements and press reviews of the world leaders showing their determination to continue the war against terrorism.

Yet in spite developments achieved during that last two decades, including destruction of Al Qaeda training bases, killing and apprehension of the most active leaders including Bin Laden, Al Zawahri, Zergawi and others Al Qaeda pattern of terrorism seems to be paralyzed. However, we are witnessing another tragedy in London trains' suicide bombing (July 2005) and Paris and many parts of the world. Therefore, only focusing terrorism leaders is not enough to eradicate their well-documented thought.

Today, for many Muslims it is becoming difficult to condemn Al Qaeda, for two reasons:

First: If anyone calls Muslims to implement sharia law and Islamic teachings in their life or addresses them by Quranic verses Muslims cannot reject his or even disagree with him.

Second: Muslims, in general, have no allegiant to their unelected governments, therefore they always show no respect to the government views. They have lost all confidence in the rulers and ruling systems, therefore governmental media and its official reports made against terrorists.

This is the situation for which Bin Landen's and so called Al-Qaeda leaders fought to a chive. In one of his speeches following September 11, Usama bin Laden swore that America and the West will never enjoy peace unless they comply with Al-Qaeda requirements contained in its war declaration.

- To face Al-Qaeda we need alternatives, including attractive and influential political leader who can address the problems of their people, new political and socio-economical solutions, address the citizens with new ideas new hope and reliability.
- Now, Al-Qaeda in not existing as an organization or group of fighters whom we can face them with fighters and air strikes. Al-Qaeda is growing now as new Islamic school of thought. It is a concept and ideology. The war against terrorism with its mistakes gave Al-Qaeda ideology tremendous support to extend throughout the world and among the young people.

Security measures and protective governmental activities in some countries is further enhancing the wide-spreading of Al-Qaeda ideology to maintain its patterns of Jihad. Teachings of Al-Qaeda may continue to spread as a religious worship, but, creating Al-Qaeda patterns of suicide terrorism.

In an informative paper assessing Al Qaeda trends in terrorism and its future potentialities, Bruce Hoffman has pointed out essential facts to be thoroughly considered in planning for future strategies of combating Al Qaeda attacks.

Vulnerability of the modern infrastructures which may be targeted by Al Qaeda, Al Qaeda efforts in recruiting Muslims living in worsening social and political environment and prolonged war against terrorism conducted by the governments in the absence of public support were among the facts emphasized by Hoffman[26(1)]. However, the attempt made by Hoffman to write obituary of Bin Laden and Al Qaeda, his failure to understand what Al Qaeda might do, and how it would, and assessing challenges facing Al Qaeda to ensure its durability as an ideology and concept; were rather uninformative. What is obvious among the Muslim –in general- Bin Laden and Al Qaeda, though not key players in the everlasting hate concept between Muslims and the West, they have indirectly achieved their goal of reviving Jihad among the Muslims and promoting hope and confidence for new generations. Ensuring durability Al Qaeda ideology was not a challenge, because Al Qaeda has no ideology, but it has developed means to activate the ideology of all Muslims maintained in Quran and Sunna. Al Qaeda and Bin Laden initiatives, strategies and methodologies are now more popular, gaining more supporters, attracting new sympathizers and developing new clandestine infrastructures that would never be detected without extended public support within the Islamic communities. Small portion of the financial resources used in war against terrorism and other security measures may change the political and social attitude of the public in Islamic countries, and develop a successful political war against terrorism.

Otherwise, time is in favor of Al Qaeda concept and mechanisms and the future is for new patterns of Al Qaeda attacks, probably, rare but might be painful to leave the West under terror all the time.

---

26 (1) **Bruce Hoffman. "Al Qaeda, Trends in Terrorism and Future potentialities: An Assessment." Studies in Conflict and Terrorism, (26) 2003.**

FOUR

MUSLIM SCHOLARS' PERSPECTIVE OF JIHAD

Muslim and Non-Muslim Scholars alike generate complex and dangerous perspectives on Islamic Jihad. This everlasting diversity of perspectives, based upon Divine commands, may become rooted in the hearts and minds of the new generations in Islamic countries and in the Western nations as well, generating perpetual hate, danger and unrest. In the following two chapters we outline and review such diverse perspectives for analysis and consideration.

Recently several Muslim scholars have issued controversial advisory opinions on Jihad and terrorism. Muslim scholars have unanimously condemned all forms of terrorism and denounced violence in general. However, Muslim scholars are of opinion that the Palestinian violence against Israel is a matter of self-defense, therefore, they tend to look at it as an issue of justice and human rights.

There is a well-grounded state of disinclination and hate between Muslims and Jews. This state of hostility is religious-oriented, generating, what for the moment appears to be a continuing clash between the two cultures. A stalwart contentment exists in both religions emphasizing that war between Muslims and Jews is an inevitable fact, and Muslims are confident that they shall be victorious one day by killing all the Jews on the earth.

Palestinian and Israeli conflict is part of a broader pattern of historical conflict, and is thus not the only issue to be settled in this part of the world. Throughout history Muslims and Jews have been hostile and lived under a state of continuous preparedness. In the context of this state of hostility, Islamic Jihad with its inclusive concept remains in Muslims' culture and strategies as a means of defense and as a form of worship determined by Quran. Therefore, it may never be settled peacefully by the two parties, unless peace is imposed upon them by the international powers. Such fact may be concluded from the various statements and views of Muslim scholars.

1. The attitude of Al-Azhar scholars

Al –Azhar as the most authenticated scientific and religious authority in the Islamic world, might be of great impact in developing and modernizing the concepts of Islamic Jihad and its rules and future perspectives in the context of the contemporary global changes. The great majority of Muslims respect explanations and religious Fatwa issued from Al-Azhar scholars. However, the controversial views adopted by individuals and statements issued under political influences, might lead to misunderstanding among the Muslims and affect the reliability of such institutions. Following are statements and writings related to Al-Azhar scholars.

- Sheikh Muhammad Sayyid Tantawi

Tantawi, Sheikh of Al-Azhar – the highest religious official in Egypt and a presidential appointee – called for Jihad against Israel "In defense of the holy places, the liberation of the land, and the repulsion of the enemy." He has stated that combating the oppression is incumbent upon the entire Islamic nation [Ummah] and not an obligation of the Palestinians alone. Sheikh Tantawi also declared that Islam requires that the leaders and people of the Arab and Islamic states should support the Jihad of the Palestinian people. Jihad in the path of Allah is a virtue that binds Muslims at all times, and it is an obligation on everyone who is able to carry it out. Tens of Qur'anic verses narrate the virtue of Jihad in the path of Allah, as well as tens of prophetic traditions [Hadiths]. Jihad to confront the enemy and liberate the pillaged land is an obligation on Muslims in every time and place. Jihad in Islam was not legislated in order to fight faithful people, or to take away their money, violate their [women's] honor, occupy their land, curtail their freedoms, or negate their dignity. Rather, the Jihad was legislated to repel the aggressor enemy, support the oppressed, exalt the word of the Allah, and to fight the vile. This is what our brothers are now doing in occupied Palestine. Their Jihad against the enemy, against oppression, and against the Israeli tyranny is a legitimate and noble Jihad. It is obligatory for the entire [Islamic] nation should. to support them in their Jihad. It is sufficient. that they are waging Jihad in the name of the entire [Islamic] nation and advancing their spirits in sacrifice to the religion of Allah and in defense of the blessed Al-Aqsa mosque. The entire [Islamic] nation should support them in the defense of their holy places and asserts their legitimate rights to [wage] Jihad to stop the enemy and the oppression which they have endured as Allah afflicted them with, and since the entire Islamic Ummah was afflicted by, what is called "Israel."

Again, in his book titled "Benoo Israel in Quran and Sunna ", Imam Mohammed Tantawy, states this issue as follows: [27(1)]

> "Arab and Islamic countries should support the Palestinian shock troops "Fedayeen" enabling them threaten Israeli security, as an introduction for the final fighting supposed to be conducted by the Muslims with the intention of purgation of the holy land from the Jews. The coming Palestine war should be based on religious Jihad rather than nationalism, because, that is the duty of all Muslims in the world".

الإمام الأكبر/ محمد سيد طنطاوي ، بنو إسرائيل في القرآن والسنة ، القاهرة: دار الشروق 2000 ، 27 ص ص 745 - 748.

-   Sheikh Ali Abu Al-Hassan, head of Al-Azhar's Religious Ruling Committee, said,

"It is the sense of danger that unites the West. They have put together a coalition against Islam. They sense danger only from Islam. This feeling has united them against a single enemy, which is Islam. Why, therefore, should we ourselves not unite? ... We, as Nation of Islam, are all targeted by our enemy why should we not unite, therefore, around the slogan of, 'There is no God but Allah and Muhammad is the Messenger of Allah' and fight our enemy?"

In the view of Sheikh Ali Abu Al-Hassan, entering into an alliance with the Americans against Afghanistan constitutes Ridah [that is, turning away from belief in Islam, for which the punishment is death, with no possibility of clemency] ... The Afghan opposition [forces] must not put [their] hand in the hand of the Americans; they must stand with their countrymen [and] their co-religionists, otherwise Allah and his angels will curse them...[2]

There is no doubt that this is a case of a hostile state fighting us, and we must resist it... Resistance in this case is by all possible means, even by means of war. If the enemy sets foot on the lands of Islam, he must be fought. In this case, a man must set out [on a Jihad] without the permission of his father, a woman without the permission of her husband, a debtor without the permission of his lender, and a slave without the permission of his master. Islam urges us to set out on a Jihad for the sake of Allah until we accomplish one of two good things: martyrdom or victory...

When Islam is attacked, there are no borders. Jihad in this instance is an obligation for all Muslims... In this instance, the aggression is against Islam and therefore it is the obligation of all Muslims, not only the local residents, to protect this piece of land.

- Dr. Abd Al-Azim Al-Mut'ani, Al-Azhar University lecturer, has stated his opinion as follows: "This war is a criminal attack, genuinely similar to the first crusader wars, which the West waged in the Middle Ages under the rallying cry of defending the Christian pilgrims, when their actual target was Islam and the Muslims. Now, the U.S. has declared a war on Afghanistan, under the rallying cry of fighting terrorism, when the actual goal is to harm Islam and to wipe it off the face of the earth…"

In another article, Al-Mut'ani discussed the differences between Jihad and terrorism:

"Terrorism is a modern term. In Islam, the meaning of terrorism is intimidation, not all intimidation is forbidden by religious law… In the modern age, when [different] kinds of oppression and persecution emerged, some ethnic groups in almost every society were stripped of their rights. When they insisted on their rights, and [when] the despotic regimes rejected them – the oppressed and persecuted found no way to express themselves but by means of [various] kinds of rebellion…"

- Dr. Abd Al-Sabour Shahin also discussed the differences between terrorism and Jihad as follows:

"The truth is that the way Islam uses the word 'terrorism' is honorable, as Allah said: 'Make ready for them whatever you can of armed strength and of mounted pickets at the frontier, whereby you may daunt the enemy of Allah and your enemy.' The terrorism mentioned in this verse refers to intimidation or threat, not necessarily to damage. For this reason, accusing Islam or Muslims of terrorism is mistaken, because Muslims as a nation are the symbol of peace in the world and the Muslim nation has never attacked a neighboring nation.

There is a huge difference between terrorism and Jihad. Jihad is a general term that includes Jihad by means of words, Jihad by means of leadership, and Jihad by means of war. War is only on behalf of the nation and in accordance with its decision, and not according to the decision of an individual. What is happening with the Palestinians is a

Jihad that is legitimate according to religious law, aimed at defending the Islamic holy places. What the Afghani people are doing in response to the aggression is also a Jihad that is legitimate according to religious law.

- Dr. Yahyah Isma'il, the official spokesman of the Al-Azhar clerics, added:

"This war is a war against Muslims and Islam. Everyone must offer help to the mujahidin brothers in Afghanistan. They should not be abandoned in the tragedy to which they are subject." In a similar vein, the Islamic Sheikh Youssef Al-Badri called on "Muslims to declare a Jihad against the Americans

- Sheik Ali Guma, Egyptian Mufti:

According to Sheik Ali Guma, Egyptian Mufti: "The one with the authority to declare Jihad is the imam who has under his [command] a regular army capable of waging a war of regular armies. When the Prophet was in Mecca, he had no army, and therefore he could not declare Jihad although that is, there was a state of hostility between Muslims and the polytheists, and there was harm caused to the believers by the polytheists, However, all the Prophet ordered his comrades to do was to say: 'You have your religion and we have our religion.'. The Prophet taught us that warfare can exist only under a flag, and that the one with the right to declare Jihad is the one with the flag. The one with the flag in our days is the president of the state, in every one of the [Muslim] countries. He, and the leaders at his side, is capable of assessing whether this war is beneficial or whether it leads to loss, whether the war will protect the Muslims or whether it will harm them. The world has let the Jews spread corruption throughout the land and they have succeeded in obtaining international legitimacy to territories that were conquered after 1967. Israel is a special case that does not exist [anywhere else] on the earth. We are facing a criminal occupation which is the source of terror the one who carries out Fedaii [martyrdom] operations against the Zionists and blows himself up suicide terrorism is, without a doubt, a Shahid, because he is defending his homeland against the occupying enemy who is supported by superpowers such as the U.S. and Britain.

Is it permitted to kill an Israeli traveling outside the borders of his land? because he is a Harbi and the Harbi spreads corruption throughout the earth.

-   Sheikh Ahmed Mahmood Karima:

In a recently published study on Islamic Jihad, professor Karima[28] has elaborated Islamic Jihad, drawing clear distinction between Jihad and terrorism as follows:

1. Terrorism in it is political or international concept as well as state terrorism is forbidden in Islam. It is also forbidden to terrify Muslims.
2. According to Islamic rules it is forbidden to terrify non-Muslim, unless he criticizes Islam.
3. It is acceptable in Islam to terrify non-Muslims, if they are fighting against Muslims directly or indirectly, provided that it should be with the permission of the regent and in gradual form and steps.
4. Fighting in Islam is defensive and its causes are emphasized in Quran as:
    -   If Muslims or their religion is attacked.
    -   Those who worship anything except Allah.
    -   Those who expel Muslims from their homes unjustly.
5. Fighting or Jihad should take place to secure the process of spreading Islam and breaching. It is most essential to fight those who tend to conspire against Islam

---

28 دراسة فقهية مقارنة – القاهرة - 2004

2. The Saudi Arabian Clerics:

On November, 2004, a communiqué calling for Jihad in Iraq was issued by twenty-six Saudi clerics who were holding positions as lecturers of Islamic studies in various government universities in Saudi Arabia[29(1)]. The signatories of the communiqué have claimed that resistance against the coalition is an Islamic duty:

> "There is no doubt that Jihad against the occupiers is an obligation upon any Muslim. This is a type of Jihad aiming to repel the aggressors from an Islamic land. Thus, there is no need for a caliph or Imam to declare Jihad in such situation. Resistance of the aggressors is a legitimate right according to the Sharia, which requires the Iraqi people to defend itself, its land, its honor and oil, just as they have resisted British colonialism in the past".

The contents of the communiqué were, repeated later in March, 2005 by a famous Saudi scholar, Sheikh Salman Al-Odeh who claimed that resistance of the occupiers in Palestine, Iraq is not considered

---

29 The 26 signatories are: Sheikh Dr. Ahmad Al-Khudhairi, Sheikh Dr. Hamed bin Ya'qub

    Al-Farih, Sheikh Dr. Al-Sharif Hatem Al-'Awni, Sheikh Khaled Al-Qasem Sheikh Dr. Saud Al-Fanisan, Sheikh Dr. Sa'id bin Naser Al-Ghamdi, Sheikh Dr. Safar bin Abd Al-Rahman

    Al-Hawali, Sheikh Dr. Salman bin Fahd Al-'Odah, Sheikh Suleiman Rashudi, Sheikh Dr. Saleh bin Muhammad Al-Sultan, Dr. Abd Al-Rahman bin 'Alush Madkhali, Sheikh Dr. Abd, Sheikh Dr. Abd Allah bin Ibrahim Al-Tariqi, Sheikh Dr. Abd Allah bin Abd Al-Aziz Al-Zayadi, Sheikh Dr. Abd Allah Wakil Al-Sheikh, Sheikh Dr. Abdul Wahab bin Naser Al-Tariri, Sheikh Dr. Ali bin Hassan Alasiri, Sheikh Dr. Ali Badahdah, Sheikh Dr. 'Awdh bin Muhammad Al-Qarni, Sheikh Dr. Qasem bin Ahmad Al-Qatradi, Sheikh Dr. Muhammad bin Hassan

    Al-Sharif, Sheikh Dr. Muhammad bin Sa'id Al-Qahtani, Sheikh Dr. Musaffar Al-Qahtani, Sheikh Dr. Mahdi Muhammad Rashad Al-Hakami, Sheikh Dr. Nasser Al-'Omar Al-Moslim.

terrorism[30(1)]. The communiqué of the twenty-six Saudi scholars was considered a serious Fatwa, which might remain as a reference. Further, in what could be one of the most significant internal challenges, Sheikh Hamoud bin Oqla Al-Shuaibi, a senior cleric, issued his fatwa just days after the Sept. 11 attacks, stating that:

> "Whoever supports the infidel against Muslims is considered an infidel ... It is a duty to wage Jihad on anyone who supports the attack on Afghanistan. Support is defined as assistance "by hand, by tongue, or by money."

A liberal Muslim scholar, Abd Al-Hamid Al-Ansari, former dean of Islamic Law in Qatar University issued a modern Fatwa on Jihad, accusing Islamist clerics with distorting the meaning of Jihad to justify the ideology of violence. Al-Ansari's Fatwa, which was published in Al-sharq Al-Awsat daily Newspaper on March, 2004 stated that:

1- "Jihad, in its true sense as defined in the Quran and as implemented by the Prophet [Muhammad] and his noble companions, is a means of defending differences, pluralism, and diversity. That is, it is [a means] of defending freedom of choice [as is written in the Quran] "There is no coercion in Islam" ... [2:256]. From the beginning, Jihad has been defined by two goals: The first was a response to aggression and oppression [as told in the Quran 22:39]. "The second [goal] is the liberation of the persecuted peoples from tyrannical regimes, as happened to the Persian and Byzantine peoples".

2- "The first ones to distort the concept of Jihad were the ancient Khawarij ['those who go out']. They rose up with arms against the righteous Imam [i.e., the Caliph 'Ali Ibn Abi Taleb] and against the virtuous society of the companions of the Prophet. The Khawarij called themselves Al-Muwahhidoun [The unifiers of God, or monotheists] and they called their movement Jihad.

---

30 www.MEMRI.org/bin

The companions of the Prophet were not deceived by these shows of piety and numerous ritual acts; they called them Khawarij and saw their actions as insurrection and rebellion.

3- "In contrast, [today] the Muslim public has been deceived by the deeds of the new Khawarij, and considers bin Laden a Jihad warrior, and his deeds as required by Jihad. Even if Muslims ostensibly condemned terrorism – the shows of rejoicing were universal and they believed that American deserved what happened to it, as a result of its subjective policy.

"During the modern era, the concept of Jihad has been distorted by the new Khawarij, those groups that took for themselves the title of Jihad. But [Jihad] against whom? Against their societies and governments. Their ideas were taken from the ideas of some Islamic thinkers such as Sayyed Qutb and [Abu A'la] Al-Mawdoudi. The perception of Jihad in the eyes of these two masters emerges from the assumption that the Muslims are the guardians of the human race, that Allah has charged them with liberating it from the tyrants on earth, and that Jihad is the only means of establishing an Islamic government that will rule the world".

The above Fatwa of Sheikh Al-Ansari was highlighted by various reactions and counter-reactions. However, it was not directly denounced by any Muslim scholar. The most senior Mufti of Saudi Arabia Sheikh Abdu Al-Aziz bin Al-sheikh commenting on the communiqué has considered presence of Americans in Iraq as an occupation despite the UN support. He left the decision of fighting those occupiers to the Iraqi Ulama, because other Ulama may not understand what is happening there on ground.

3. The attitude of other Muslim scholars

- Sheikh Yousuf Al-Qaradhawi

Sheik Yousf Al –Qaradhawi, the president the Muslim scholar's union, says:

"it is the duty of all Muslims to support Palestinian suicide bombers, become they are defending themselves and their land. Fighting Americans in Iraq is the duty of all Muslims because they are occupying an Islamic land[31]

Martyrdom operations in Palestine constitutes legitimate resistance. It is the defense of their religion, land soul, property and honor.

"our hearts bleed for the attacks that has targeted the world Trade Center [WTC], as well as other institutions in the United States despite our strong oppositions to the American biased policy towards Israel on the military, political and economic fronts. Islam, the religion of tolerance, holds the human soul in high esteem, and considers the attack against innocent human beings a grave sin, this is backed by the Qur'anic verse which reads: 'who so ever kills a human being [as punishment] for [crimes] other than manslaughter or [sowing] corruption in the earth, it shall be as if he has killed all mankind, and who so ever saves the life of one, it shall be as if he had saved the life of all mankind' (Al-Ma'idah:32)."

Although Shiekh Al-Qaradahaw, has started recently, to amend his previous Fatwas and statements pertaining to the requirement of the International Community, still, the radical statements he issued during 2004 remain as an encouraging element for the extremists. Such Fatwa's included permitting the killing of "fetuses" (unborn) Jews, because (according to him) when Jews are born and grown-up they will join the Israeli army. Furthermore, on September 3, 2004, (at the Egyptian Journalist Union) Al- Qaradawi issued a fatwa to kill all American civilians working in Iraq. And on July 3, 2004, he issued

---

31 2.9.2004 ،1371 العدد ،أخبار العرب

another fatwa permitting the killing of Muslim intellectuals as being apostates, claiming that Islam justifies the killing of such apostates.

- Sheikh Hassen Al-Turabi

Sheikh Hassen Al-Turabi one of the key players in the contemporary Islamic movement has stated two controversial definitions of Jihad. In his book titled Politics and Governance he defines Jihad as follows [32] :

> "Jihad, when it is necessary for political reformation is heated by instigation and abetment and pushed forward by social injustice as well as the threat imposed by polytheists. Such situation causes ground for revolution against bad governance. However, if the revolutionary Jihad exceed beyond the victory, it becomes fatal and damaging, if not supported by the pious and righteous persons. Thus, Jihad may go further to prejudice the peace and eradicate the others".

In the same book, Turabi gives another controversial definition of Jihad when he says:

> "In general, Jihad – when it is urgent – is a method of self-defense against the aggressors. Jihad is not a means of spreading religion by force, because we believe that people, normally find the right path by their hearts and develop intimacy, peace informing and choice by the sake of Allah, in the context of freedom, honesty and willingness. Jihad should not be authorized unless there an abnormal threat of aggression. Following the victory of Mujahidin peace and freedom should prevail among all parties of the fighting".

---

32 حسن الترابي – السياسة والحكم : النظم السلطانية بين الأصول وسنن الواقع – بيروت – دار الساقي 2004

In fact, what Turabi is defining may a political violence because he is referring to Jihad against a government. To reform a political system by revolting against the government may not be considered as Jihad. Turabi also calls for Jihad if there is and aggression, without mentioning who is the aggressor.

Turabi considers Jihad due to his personal experience within the Sudan. In practice, just before the salvation coup of 1989, Turabi had been calling his followers for Jihad against the elected government, because he thought that the Sudan government was about to abolish the sharia law for the sake of peace agreement with the southern Sudan. Following the salvation coup Trabi declared authorized and encouraged Jihad against Sudanese people in the Southern and Eastern parts of the country. Latter, when he lost his political power in ruling parting, Turabi clearly declared that fighting in the southern Sudan is not Islamic Jihad. Consequently, Turabi started negotiation with the Southern leaders for a peaceful settlement.

- Sheikh Abdullah Algadiry

According to Al Gadiry[33], objective of Jihad are as follows:

o Establish Islamic system of life on the earth.
o Self-defense against aggression of non-believers.
o To gain shahada for the cause of Allah.
o To purify Islamic communities from corruption and the hypocrites.
o Follow the messengers path.
o Realize the globalization of Islam, as determined in the Quran:

"Blessed is he who sent down the criterion of right and wrong, to his slave Muhammed, that he may be warner to the mankind."[34]

---

33 ‏1992،عبدالله القادري، الجهاد في سبيل الله، جدة، المنارة.
34 Surat al Furqan, verse 1.

- Muhammed Kheir Heikal

Mohamed Heikal, has classified fighting in Islam into (6) types, showing the types that are considered as Jihad according to Sharia as follows:

1. Fighting recessives or renegades, is Jihad.
2. Fighting citizens who rebel against their governments or attempt coupe, is not Jihad.
3. Fighting citizens who wage internal wars or use force to realize political objectives, is not Jihad.
4. Fighting these who are involved in armed robberies and street gangs is Jihad.
5. Fighting disbelievers for self-defense to protect property, life or freedom is Jihad; is Jihad.
6. Fighting against the rulers and legal government is not Jihad as far as the ruler is Muslim and applying Islamic rules.[35]

- Sheikh Muhamed Al-Mamoon Al -Hudhaiby

In October, 2003, Mohamed Al-Hudhaiby, issued a statement supporting the Palestinian upraise on the occasion of the 3rd year of "intifada" celebration. According to Al-Hudhaiby, the uprising (intifada) performed by the Palestinians is one of the most important roles of Islamic Jihad, therefore, It is obligatory for all Muslims to support such patterns of Jihad.[36]

- Sheikh Muhamed Tahir Al- Qadri

Muhammad Tahir Al-Qadri, a prominent Pakistani scholar has drawn a distinction between terrorism and Jihad as follows:

---

35 1993 محمد خير هيكل ، الجهاد والقتال في الإسلام في السياسة الشرعية ، بيروت: دار البيارق.
36 Mohamed Al Mamoon Al Hudhaiby, Arab New, newspaper no 1041, issued Oct. 3, 2003.

"The killing of innocent people is terrorism. Attacking human religious, political, social and cultural rights is also terrorism"[37]. Jihad and terrorism have no relation with each other nor is there anything in common between them. On the other hand, Jihad stands for the eradication of terrorism. Jihad-bil-qital is characterized by ending terrorism. But if! threats are posed to human life, properly and honor, fighting for defending these areas is called Jihad.

It is not meant for grabbing wealth. Expansionist designs have nothing to do with the Islamic concept of Jihad. Every charter of Human Rights terms taking up of arms against injustice and unwanted blood-letting, crushing down of rebellion and revolt, uprooting of conspiracies, violence and mischief-mongering as not only being legal but also making it binding. All that is done with a view to making the earth safe. When any individual or party transgresses its limits and encroaches upon believers to wage Jihad, so that mischief-mongering is halted and peace comes to our planet, earth.

The concept of Jihad is one of the highly misunderstood Islamic concepts. Unfortunately, the West sees it as mere fighting against disbelief and the West. While some extremist religious groups who declare their activities as Jihad, are presenting Islam in a fanatic and emotional way giving a distorted picture of Islam. So the West has wrongly conceived terrorist activities as Islamic Jihad. Islamic concept of Jihad has absolutely no link with terrorism, extremism or barbarism. Jihad means struggle for good and elimination of evil. The spiritual struggle for self-purification of the soul is the greatest Jihad declared by Prophet Mohammad (PBUH). This is known as Al-Jihad Al-Akbar. According to the Prophet's tradition this is an exclusive struggle for moral excellence, ethical perfection and spiritual purification of mankind.

-    Sheikh Muzammil Sidiqi:

---

37 www.mediamonitors.net

Sheikh Muzammil Sidiqi, of the Islamic Society of North America is a highly Harvard educated influential Imam, who serves on several boards of Muslim groups. He is counted as a nice and moderate Muslim in highest levels of leadership in the American Muslim Community. In a 2003 Fatwa, Sidiqi made the following statement:

> "I believe that as Muslims, we should participate in the system to safeguard our interests and try to bring about gradual changes. We must not forget that Allah's rules have to be established in all lands, and our efforts should lead in that direction".

In another occasion Sidiqi said:

> "America has to learn, if you remain on the side of injustice, the wrath of God will come".

The above statements of Sheikh Sidiqi are not unique. The general meaning of Sidiqi words focuses on injustice and role of America in the prevailing injustice in many parts of the world, where violence is generated. This type of accusation which is growing among Muslims the official Media in Islamic countries, which intentionally tends to develop state of hate between people and the west, as excuse for governments.

4. The attitude of Islamic groups:

The history of Islam has witnessed innumerable religious groups known as Al-Firaq Al-Islamiya, holding controversial views on several religious issues. Holding such controversial views was highly appreciated during the early Islamic era, because Muslims were in need of understanding Quran and Sunna and establishing rules for different aspects of life which were not detailed during the life of the Prophet. Thereafter, the groups went far away from their objectives by being involved in depth in very minor issues leading to fighting[38].

.كرم محمد زهدي وآخرين ، تفجيرات الرياض :الأحكام والآثار ، القاهرة ، 2003 38

This trend of grouping, although, it is inconsistency with democracy and requirements of freedom of expression, illiteracy and unfavorable political situation in the Islamic countries may remain as a cause of worsening the impact of such groups in the life of the Muslims. Among such groups known to have views in contemporary Jihad and terrorism are:

- Al-Jamaa Al-Islamiya:

The Egyptian Islamic group (Al-Jamaa Al-Islamiya) has published recently two books denouncing violence against random civilian targets and condemning the terroristic activities performed by Egyptian Islamic groups. The two books written by eight of the leaders of Egyptian Islamic group contain new advisory opinions and new explanations of Jihad rules and principles[39]. The writers are leaders of Egyptian Islamic group who were recently released from prisons including:

- Karam Mohamed Zuhdi.
- Ali Mohamed Ali Al Asharif.
- Hamdi Abdul Rahman Abdul Azeem.
- Assim Abdul Majid Muhammad.
- Najih Ibrahim Abu Auah.
- Usama Ibrahim Hafiz.
- Fuad Muhammad Al Dawalibi.
- Muhammad Issam Al Deen Darbale.

- Al-Qaeda and associates:

In 1998, a joint fatwa issued by Usama Bin Laden, Ayman Al-Zawahiri, Abu-Yasir Taha, Mir Hamzah and Fazlur Rahman, included:

"The ruling to kill the Americans and their allies-civilians and military – is an individual duty for every Muslim who can do it in any country in which it is

---

39 الجماعة الإسلامية ، المراجعة الفقهية.

possible to do it, in order to liberate Al-Aqsa Mosque and the Holy Mosque [Mecca] from their grip, and in order for their armies to move out of all the lands of Islam, defeated and unable to threaten any Muslim. This is an accordance with the words of Almighty Allah, "and fight the Pagans all together as they fight you all together," and "fight them until there is no more tumult or oppression, and there prevail justice and faith in Allah".

- The Republican Islamic Party Concept of Jihad:

It is worthy to single-out her of Jihad, because it is unique, and well accepted among a large group of dignitaries in the Islamic world, who are unable to proclaim or contribute in such unique understanding, due to lack of freedom of expression in the field. The founder and philosopher of the party, Mahmood Taha was sentenced by capital punishment in Sudan as apostate, because of his audacious interpretations of Quran. However, followers of Taha are distributed throughout the world and attempting to spread their new interpretations of Islam with the intention of bridging the gap between Islam and the West for peace and security. The Republican Islamic Party concept of Jihad was outlined by Omer Al Gariai in his book titled "Al Jihad Am Huriyat Al Eateqad" "Jihad or Freedom of Belief". Deeply emphasizing the distinction between the Quranic verses of the fundamentals (Al-Ussul) and those of the aesthetic (Al-Furoua), Al-Garai states the following views[40]:

- Jihad was a temporary Islamic legislation, because it was authorized aesthetic Quranic verses and by the verses of the fundamentals.
- Even when Jihad was authorized during the 7th century, it was not a matter of revenge or bloodshed, but it was a declared fighting adopted with ethics and humanitarian rules.

---

40 (1) 1995 ، عمر القراي ، الجهاد أم حرية الاعتقاد.

- The terroristic operations performed today under the slogans of Islamic Jihad, has nothing to do with Islam. They are mere crime against humanity and Islam as religion of peace.
- Muslim scholars have mistakenly attempted to justify Jihad of 7th century as a self-defense; however, it was not a self-defense. It was a real Jihad authorized by Quran as fighting for the cause of Allah, to raise his word on the land. Thus, Muslims fought in Asia and Europe and occupied nations. Today waging wars to spread Islam may not be accepted by the international community, which tends to live in peace and freedom.
- Jihad of the 7th century has generated certain customs, such as slavery and trafficking in persons (war prisoners) which are denounced by the international community today.

Today Muslim scholars throughout the Arab countries insist that Jihad should continue against the non-believers, until the last day. They consider everyone who does not govern with Sharia is Kafir. In fact, they agree with the so-called Mujahidin of today in all Quranic verses of Jihad as it is without developed interpretations. Therefore, it is not easy to stop new generation from becoming terrorists.

- The universal Muslim movement

In 2001 the universal Muslim Movement for the Advancement of Humanity known as Ummah based in UK, issued a "Fatwa" to explain its own point of view on Islamic Jihad. Emphasizing the duty and necessity of global Jihad, the Fatwa sponsored by Ummah gives answers to the main three questions related to Jihad as follows:

- The Muslim Ummah and suffering humanity, now subject to total subjugation by the Occident, shackled by the economic, political and military yoke requires an answer. This hegemony is implemented by client regimes who have no conscience for the peoples they misrule. Capitalism as feudalism is and injustice. Therefore, we have no option but to engage in Jihad. All men and women have a duty to themselves and others to remove the yoke imposed upon us.

- It is incumbent upon all Muslims to enlist as Mujahidin, to support in every way the Mujahidin if they are not able to perform Jihad themselves. Muslims should make common cause with suffering humanity.

- Authority for Jihad is The Quran, and the example of the Noble Prophet. Au God conscious peoples shall join revolution without borders to adopt one earth, one humanity under one God. All global infrastructure beneficial to the oppressors is legitimate target for the wrath of the people and divine justice.

- In the absence of the caliphate or a global Islamic unified institution, it falls upon Ummah Movement to make a declaration to call the oppressed to arms and Jihad. [41]

In a moderate exposition of the concept of Jihad, Yusuf Ibish stated:

"The Greater Jihad is fighting one's animal tendencies. It is internal rather than external; striving in the path of God to overcome one's animal side. Man share with animal certain characteristics which, if let loose, make him a very dangerous beast. To bring these passions under control, that is what Jihad means. Man has a tendency to overestimate his spiritual potentials. He has a tendency to control and exploit his environment and other human beings. Jihad is essential against such tendencies. The Lesser Jihad- according to Yusuf- fighting on behalf of the community, in its defense- is a duty incumbent on Muslim, provided that he is attacked. A man has the right to defend his life, his property, and he has to organize himself along these lines. It is true that Muslims have waged wars, wars in

---

41 Umma, Islamic Edicts (fatwa), Vol. 1, Understanding Islam series No. 5, Nun Eaton Unity Publications. 2001

ordinary sense. But this indicates that some Muslims have not exercised the greater Jihad.[42]

Noah Feldman, professor at New York University with a doctorate degree is Islamic thought from Oxford has dealt with issue of Jihad in a unique and rather constructive way. Feldman, understanding the way of thinking of many moderate Muslims, wrote his book titled; After Jihad: America and the struggle for Islamic Democracy [43]

The prophet, upon whom be prayers and peace, was returning from one of their battles, when he said, "you have made the finest of returns; you have returned from the lesser Jihad to the greater Jihad." They said, "And what is the greater Jihad?"

He answered, "Man's struggle against his desires".

Starting his work with the above famous words of Prophet Muhammad – prayers and peace be upon him – Feldman attempted to call for encouraging the great majority of the moderate Muslims to enhance causes of the greater Jihad as a means to overcome the growing ideology of violence, attributed to Jihad.

"There are still some prepared to do violence in the name of Islam, who will doubtless make continued attempts to terrorize the West. But many, perhaps most, Muslims are, instead, entering a confirmed period of post-Jihad, "post" in the sense that the option of holy war now seems spent, peripheral, unrealistic, and indeed distasteful in the light of the violence of September 11. They are turning toward another kind of Jihad that is embedded in Islamic thought and tradition, a type of Jihad explicated in the well-known hadith that forms the epigraph. In one version of this received tradition, the Prophet Muhammad preceded a band of his followers in the return from a battle against the infidel. Observing the battle-weary Muslims approaching camp, the Prophet delivered a sobering message: you have returned from the lesser Jihad to embark upon the greater Jihad.

---

42 Quoted in A.G. Noorani, Islam & Jihad – Prejudice Versus Reality. London: Zed Book. 2002, P.46

43 Noah Feldman. After Jihad: America and the struggle for Islamic Democracy, New York, Farra, Straus and Giroux. 2003

In the orthodox interpretation of the anecdote, incorporated in some versions of the tradition, the greater Jihad is the inward struggle to perfect one's moral qualities. Sufi mystics have long embraced this interpretation, which they extend to mean that life's central task lies in overcoming the ego.

More broadly, inward Jihad means any worthy struggle infused by the principles of religion. One might say it was this more general type of struggle that the Prophet described as the greater Jihad, as opposed to the lesser Jihad of actual war. Jihad can also mean, then, by association, Islam's struggle to create a just system of political government. After all, the Muslims whom the Prophet addressed were returning to the bosom of their community, presumably to take up its affairs".

Feldman suggests democratization of Islamic states as a workable strategy to turn Muslims from political violence to participate in electoral politics; with the historical roots of democracy available in Islam.

So. Contrary to what is sometimes believed in the U.S.; Islam is not inherently committed to the overthrow of Western ideals. To the contrary, many, though by no means all, Muslims find the combination of Islamic ideals and democratic values appealing. Today Muslims around the world embrace the elegance, logic, and depth of Islam perhaps more warmly than at any time in a century. In Islam's language of justice, morality, hope, and commitment, they find not only religion, but a vital force in the realms of politics, society, and the spirit. At the same time, as their reliance on Islam grows, Muslims are also embracing the ideals of self-government and freedom associated with democracy. To an increasing number of Muslims, these democratic values resonate with Islam and can develop in tandem with it. Wherever advocates have been free to speak out or run for office in the name of Islamic democracy, they have found an eager audience.

Feldman, however, seems to be anxious about the reality of the future of Islamic democracy and it impact on the great majority of Muslims upon whom strict religious dictates of Islamic law might be enforced through policing of personal religious practices. In fact, democracy is democracy whatever it is the religion of the voters. If democracy is practiced in an Islamic society, no doubt it will reflect Islamic values in the context of the modern global environment.

Democracy is not new in history, but the mechanism may be improved to meet the needs of the present Islamic communities.

In parallel with this, Muslim scholars are also exploring arguments to prove the innocence of Islam from any terroristic accusations. For instance, according to Shukri,[44(1)] in the Quran, the Arabic terms "Rahba" meaning terror and its derivatives appears eight times, and only once it is used in the sense of scaring the enemies of Allah and the believers during "Jihad". This is shown in the Quranic verse which reads as follows:

"Against them make ready your strength to the utmost of your powers including steeds of war to strike terror into the hearts of the enemies of Allah and your enemies."[45(2)]

In the other seven instances as quoted by Shukri, "rahba" is used solely to call for the fear of Allah. However, the dilemma facing Muslim scholars today is not only to claim the absence of the term terror in the main sources of Islam, but to also explain the concept of Jihad which is repeatedly affirmed by the Holy Quran, and to prove that Islamic Jihad is not a model of contemporary terrorism. Contemporary Muslim scholars are almost all influenced by political organizations, and in consequence their span of analysis tends to be limited due to political influence and pressures imposed by different religious factions, who are prepared to issue decrees that might disqualify any Muslim scholar who attempts to raise issues outside of a narrow perspective. From this point, we may draw four broad themes for discussion.

Firstly; Islam as a religion and in the quality of its teachings and principles are well accepted and appreciated even by disbelievers throughout the world. There is no need to be apologetic about Islam.

---

44 Muhammad Aziz Shukri, International Terrorism: A legal critique. Vermont: Amana Books, 1991.

45 Surah (8), verse (60).

Secondly, many Muslim scholars repeatedly emphasize Islamic rules, principles, guidelines as most appropriate to organize human behaviour and realize justice and social well fair. However, in this respect they draw on models of the very old Islamic history. However, they never discuss the present situation of the Muslims. They are avoiding the contemporary behavior of Muslims which is of course the concern of the international community. Today, there is no specific Islamic state or community that can be taken as a successful guiding module to encourage other communities.

Why Muslims of today are so different from their historical ancestors? Why do they tend to violence? Why do they hate others? Why are the Muslims of today classified into extremists, fanatics and secularists? Who is authorized to speak on behalf of Muslims? Who is responsible for the deteriorating psychological, political, social and economic situation of Muslims throughout the world? Many such questions remain without answer

Thirdly, there are problems related to the definition of Islamic states their existence and their realities in the context of the modern global system and legality. In this respect, most controversial is the issue of the relations between the present ruling regimes of the so called Islamic states and their citizens. Who is to be blamed for the illegal acts of the Muslims? What are the current Islamic states' responsibility for the behaviour of the individuals?

The term Islam can be translated into English as "Submission" or "Obedience" to the law, as expressed in Qur'an.[46] The term Muslim can be translated as that person who obeys Allah according to the teachings and orders embodied in Qur'an and "Sunna". In this context, we know that within any group, leadership is a critical variable in determining the nature and direction that group influences might have. Thus, we might say that the Muslims are committed to Allah and they are subject to any action of authority to obey that authority or leadership. Of clear relevance here are the realities associated with the quality of leadership

---

46 Maxwell Taylor, The Fanatics: A behavioral approach to Political Violence. Extern: Brassy's, 1991.

in the present Islamic countries and among the Muslim communities, where terroristic activities or Jihad issues are generated.

Following the 2nd world war, Islamic countries developed a controversial or unacceptable patterns of political and religious leadership. Perhaps, that was due to political and socio-economic factors, but in addition the notable support of the western industrial countries. Consequently, Muslims have lost a uniform and acceptable religious authority that organizes and controls the general behaviour of the new generation in the so called Islamic states. Because of this, innumerable leaders and unqualified Muslim scholars have emerged. These scholars explain the Qur'an and issue legal advice as "Fatwa" in most critical religious issues; this has now become a normal practice of religious leaders and individual Muslim scholars. Notably, calling for Jihad within the Islamic countries and against the disbelievers has been emphasized by such groups and politically oriented religious factions. Accordingly, it might be argued that an urgent task is to start to develop the political and socio-economical settings in the Islamic countries, making way for new political and religious leaders who have the capacity to conciliate between Islamic teachings and the requirements of the contemporary international legality, and avoid internal and external conflicts. Exemplary Islamic leaders that might stand as a peacemaker are needed, to settle disputes between Muslims before they generate violence.

Fourthly: Who are the disbelievers in the Islamic perspective and who are the enemies of Islam, against whom Muslims are asked to fight for Allah's Cause? Who is supposed to sponsor Jihad in the absence of Islamic state? Is it open to every individual to call for Jihad and sponsor "Mujahidin", as well as selecting the targets of Jihad?

FIVE

NON-MUSLIM SCHOLARS PERSPECTIVE OF JIHAD

Previous studies

Measuring and understanding the impact of terrorism: a study conducted by a group of experts headed by "Larry Artery" and "David Keane" of the University of London in 2014. This study presented a comparison of the trends of terrorism between 2012 and 2013, defining the risks of terrorism and evaluating the effects of terrorist operations on the economy in countries experiencing internal conflicts and those without internal conflicts. The study examined the most dangerous terrorist groups, namely the Islamic State ISIS, Boko Haram, Al-Qaeda, the Taliban and foreign fighters in Syria. The study presented a presentation of the most (50) horrific terrorist operations, with an explanation of terrorist methods and their innovations. The study documented that the number of victims of terrorism between 2000 and 2014 has increased five times. The study, which was guided by the opinion of (25) Muslim jurists, included the following facts:

- The most effective strategies for combating terrorism since the sixties were security operations or political settlements, which led to the termination of (80%) of terrorist organizations (10%) of which achieved their goals.

- Despite the different causes and factors leading to terrorism, there are some common social and economic factors. However, the countries most exposed to terrorism in the world have common characteristics, which are:

  o Internal social hostility between ethnicities.
  o The existence of terrorism and state violence represented in political assassinations and human rights violations.
  o A high degree of violence, crime and organized conflict.

- The study revealed (13) countries that are politically, economically and socially prepared to be exposed to terrorism, namely Angola, Ivory Coast, Iran, Ethiopia, Israel, Uganda, Mali, Mexico, Bangladesh and Myanmar.

- Intentional killings claimed more lives than terrorism, as it reached (437000) people during 2012 compared to (11,000) victims of terrorism.

- Most of the victims of terrorist operations in 2013 (66%) were omitted by four Islamic groups: The Islamic State, Boko Haram, Al-Qaeda and the Taliban, which claim the Wahhabi approach, but with different visions and goals. Such fact requires moderate Muslim scholars to move and confront these groups with a clear Islamic thought.

- Encyclopedia of Eastern Wars: The involvement of the United States in the Persian Gulf, Afghanistan and Iraq, by Spencer Tucker, a book of five volumes, is one of the most important references that documented the roots of tactical wars or proactive wars. The book monitors the minute details of the American intervention in the Middle East and southern Central Asia, during the twentieth century and the twenty-first century, starting with the war between Iran and Iraq during the years 1980 and 1988. This documented encyclopedia contains pictures, evidence and intelligence reports. The highlights tactical American role in igniting and investing in Middle Eastern wars in several ways, including malicious and deceptive ones, and what confirms the lack of American intelligence understanding of many of the natures of the peoples of this region.

- In an attempt to justify the American role, the encyclopedia cites reports that have recently clarified their invalidity and talk about terrorist threats that did not exist, but which paved the way for their existence, emergence and development, sometimes intentionally and sometimes due to ignorance. This encyclopedia reinforces the hypotheses adopted by this research regarding the specificity of the region's treating terrorism and the failure to follow the plans drawn by Western countries to confront terrorism.

- Study by Robert Spencer, titled the Complete Infidel's Guide to the Quran is one of the most critical studies, having great impact on deepening the hatred of Muslims and the Islamic religion in the Western communities. The study deals with analysis, statement and criticism of the Holy Qur'an, focusing on the verses of threats to the infidels and Jews, and Prophet Muhammad promising them of punishment in this world and the hereafter. Spencer has selected (75) topics addressed by the Koran, focusing on verses that call for Jihad and fighting the infidels and the Jews.

This study, and others that dealt with Islam and Islamic Jihad in the aftermath of Al-Qaeda's attacks on the United States in 2001, present a challenge to Islamic jurists and scholars. As we have already mentioned, the numerous studies and research carried out in the Western countries and published on a large scale during the period from 2001 to 2016 on terrorism have left terrorism far away and focused on Islam and Muslims. During this period, we witnessed the trend of researchers in the Western countries towards reading the Qur'an, scrutinizing its noble verses, and communicating with Muslim scholars to clarify the meanings and objectives of the Qur'anic verses, so their published works came as a war against Islam and placing responsibility on Muslims. Perhaps the most important thing that should be done now is to refer to what was written about the role of Islam and Muslims in Western studies and to benefit from them in dealing with terrorism and cooperating with the international community.

The discipline of the study of Jihad is a new development among the Western scholars. It was focused only during the last ten years, and particularly following September 11, 2001. Unfortunately, even among the Muslim scholars, the discipline of the study of Jihad in its global context has never been thoroughly highlighted. Muslims –in general- used to recite Quranic verses related to Jihad with its original senses and its victorious concept accompanied with its historical miracles of early Islamic era. Thus, strengthening their religious belief in Jihad, they have not attempted to think of its practice in the context of the contemporary conflicts. Muslim scholars, being enclosed by the traditional sources of Jihad, have never attempted to study Jihad as a contemporary issue that might be annoying for the international community. However, when Jihad was recently linked with terrorism, Muslim scholars has endeavored to face the western offensive against Jihad with different views and contradicting explanations. They have failed to come up with a unanimous understanding to justify Jihad objectives.

Innumerable books, articles and conference papers were made available in a short period. However, such literature was not constructive and could not generate favorable elements that might bridge the gap between Muslim and non-Muslim scholars. Non-Muslims scholars dealing with the issue of Jihad, only through what they are witnessing today, and Muslims scholars as well, dealing with Jihad, only by rewriting history of Jihad as a religious worshipping, without going deep into the changing world; both were unable to arrive to a common understanding of Jihad.

Several non-Muslim scholars involved in terrorism researches has contributed in the field, by raising debatable views and highlighting their perspectives of Islamic Jihad. Among the non-Muslim scholars there are those who faithfully conveyed the history, objectives and principles of Islamic Jihad to the West, better than Muslim scholars.

However, few non-Muslim writers were rather offensive; they were extremists, with religious attitudes similar to that of radical Islamists:

1. The attitude of non-Muslim extremists:

Several non-Muslim scholars may be classified as extremists holding anti-Islamic ideologies. Views of the extremists are as follows:

- Boaz Gaynor:

Gaynor looks at Jihad as a pattern of Arab terrorism. He wrote:

> "The Islamic Jihad is one of the most complex and dangerous of the Arab terrorist organizations, with cells in many Middle Eastern countries and, apparently, in Europe as well. These groups generally act on their own initiative without coordination, sometimes even within the same country. All these groups share a fundamentalist Islamic Ideology which espouses holy war (Jihad) against the infidels, and which is under the powerful ideological-religious influence of the Islamic revolution in Iran. The Iranian regime and the Islamic Jihad groups collaborate closely at times. Some groups not only received aid guidance from Iran, but also enjoy generous support from other Arab and Islamic countries such as Libya, Syria, Sudan, Afghanistan, Pakistan, Saudi Arabia, and the Persian Gulf oil states. They also cooperate extensively with diverse Palestinian Organizations."[47(1)]

- William Boykin:

---

47 http://www.jcpa.org/j1/saa31.htm.

William Jerry Boykin, a famous extremist and U.S.A Army Lt. General made a set of remarks against Islam and Muslims. In his nomination to the new post in 2002, Boykin stated:

> "Radical Islamists" hate the U.S. because we're a Christian nation and the enemy is a guy named Satan. Satan wants to destroy this nation. He wants to destroy us as nation and as a Christian army. "Why do they hate us? The answer to that is because we're a Christian nation. We are hated because we are a nation of believers.

I knew my God was bigger than his. I knew that my God was a real God and his was an idol. Boykin was referring to a Muslim Somali warlord. He spoke about how his belief in Christianity has trumped Muslim and other non-Christians in battle. Casting the war on terrorism in religious terms, he said "Our spiritual enemy will only be defeated if we come against them in the name of Jesus". Boykin has described himself as a warrior in the kingdom of God and invited others to join with him in fighting for the U.S. through repentance, prayer and the exercise of faith in God.[48(1)]

- Moshe Sharon:

Another non-Muslim extremist wrote:

> "The war started a long time ago between two civilizations – between the civilizations based on the bible and between the civilizations based on The Quran. And this must be clear. Let me explain the difference. The bible is the creation of the spirit of a nation over a very, very long period, if we talk from the point of view of the scholar. But there is one thing that is important in the bible. It leads to salvation in two ways in Judaism; it leads to national salvation – not just a nation that

---

48 http://www.Islam-online.net/English/New/2003-10/17/article06.shtml.

wants to have a state, but a nation that wants to serve God. That's the idea behind the Hebrew text of the bible. The New Testament that took the Hebrew bible moves us towards personal salvation. So we have got these two kinds of salvation, which from time to time, meet each other.

Let's look, then, at the difference between these three religions. Judaism speaks about national salvation – namely that at the end of the story, when the world becomes a better place, Israel will be in its own land, ruled by its own king and serving God. Christianity speaks about the idea that every single person in the world can be saved from his sins, while Islam speaks about ruling the world. I can quote here in Arabic, but there is no point in quoting Arabic, so let me quote a verse in English. "Allah sent Mohammad with the true religion so that it should rule over all the religions."

The idea, then, is not that the whole world would become a Muslim world at this time, but that the whole world would be subdued under the rule of Islam. When the Islamic Empire was established in 634 AD, within seven years – 640 – the core of the Empire was created. The rules that were taken from the Quran and from the tradition that was ascribed to the Prophet Mohammad were translated into a real legal system. Jews and Christians could live under Islam provided they paid poll tax and accepted Islamic superiority. Of course, they had to be humiliated. And Jews and Christians living under Islam are humiliated to this very day.

Mohammad did accept the existence of all the Biblical Prophets before him. However, he also said that all these Prophets were Muslims. Abraham was a Muslim. In fact, Adam himself was the first Muslim. Isaac and Jacob and David and Solomon and Moses and Jesus were all Muslims, and all of them had writings similar to the Quran. Therefore, world history is Islamic history because all the heroes of history were Muslims.

Furthermore, Muslims accept the fact that each of these Prophets brought with him some kind of a revelation. Moses, brought the Taurat, which is the Torah, and Jesus brought the Injeel, which is the Evangeline or Gospel – namely the New Testament. Why then is the Bible not similar to the Quran? Mohammad explains that the Jews and Christians forged their books. Had they not been changed and forged, they would have been identical to the Quran. But because Christians and Jews do have some truth, Islam concedes that they cannot be completely destroyed by war. Nevertheless, the laws are very clear – Jews and Christians have no rights whatsoever to independent existence. They can live under Islamic rule provided they keep to the rules that Islam promulgates for them.

What happens if Jews and Christians do not want to live under the rules of Islam? Then Islam has to fight them and this fighting is called Jihad. Jihad means war against those people who do not want to accept Islamic superior rule. That is Jihad. They may be Jews; they may be Christians; they may be Polytheists. But since we do not have too many polytheists left, at least not in the Middle East – their war is against the Jews and Christians.

Any territory that comes under Islamic rule cannot be de-Islamized. Even if at one time or another, the [Non-Muslim] enemy takes over the territory that was under Islamic rule, it is considered to be perpetually Islamic. This is why whenever you hear about the Arab/ Israeli conflict; you hear territory, territory, and territory. There are other aspects to the conflict, but territory is highly important.

The Christian civilization has not only been seen as a religious opponent, but as a dam stopping Islam from achieving its final goal for which it was created. Islam was created to be the army of God, the army of Allah. Every single Muslim is a soldier in this army. Every single Muslim that dies in fighting for the spread of Islam is a Shaheed (martyr) no matter how he dies, because – and this is very important – this is an eternal word between the two civilizations. It is not a war that stops. This because it was created by Allah. Islam must be the ruler. This is a war that will not end.

Peace in Islam can exist only within the Islamic world; peace can only be between Muslim and Muslim. With the Non-Muslim world or Non-Muslim opponents, there can be only one solution – a cease-fire until Muslims can gain more power. It is an internal war until the end of days. Peace can only come if the Islamic side wins. The two civilizations can only have periods of cease-fire. And this idea of cease-fire is based on a very important historical precedent".

2. The views of the other non-Muslim scholars:

- Gilles Keppel:[49]

In his book titled; Jihad: The Trail of Political Islam, Keppel has started and concluded his study of Jihad focusing basically on the writings and views of the Muslim scholars who had dominated the 1960s, namely, Sayyad Qutb of Egypt, Abu Alaala Mawdudi of Pakistan and Al-Khomeini of Iran, whom Keppel has considered as the original theorists of the modern Islamism. Without explaining what he meant by the term Jihad, Keppel discussed the activities of several Islamic groups as well as politically-oriented Islamic movements in Islamic countries such as Algeria, Iran, Sudan, Malaysia and Pakistan.

Although Keppel has visited those countries where he noted that the Sharia – driven governments have tempered, he could not convey to his readers the real situation and attitude of the citizens in those countries. He has focused only on the activities of the governmental organizations and political parties in power. This is one of the common mistakes among the Western circles. They have been looking to the Islamic world through the same narrow windows and limited official channels. The Western circles would never understand the reality and arrive to fair judgments, unless they examine the views of the great majority of Muslims who are remaining as bystanders of what is going around.

- David Cook:

---

49 Gilles Keppel, Jihad: The Trail of Political Islam. Translated by Anthony E. Robert, London: I.B. Tauris, 2004.

The field of the study of Islamic Jihad was enriched by the tremendous contribution of David Cook[50], Professor of religious studies at Rice University, by his work titled Understanding Jihad. Cook treated Islamic Jihad very fairly tracing its history, defining its religious concept and objectives, crystallizing Jihad theory at the beginning of Islamic era, the renewal of nineteenth century, contemporary Jihad and globalist radical Islam of today. Cook noted that Muslim history began with the Prophet Mohammad's emigration to Medina as the first conquest and innovation of Jihad, which extended to series of campaigns classified into four groups:

- The battles of Badr (624), Uhud (625), Khandaq (627), Mecca (630) and Hunayn (630) which were undertaken with the goal of dominating the main areas of Hijaz, Mecca, Medina and Al-Taif.
- Raids against the Bedouin to stop their attacks against Muslims.
- Attack against Jewish tribes to secure the areas in which they reside.
- Two raids against the Byzantines at Al-Mu'ta, Tabuk and Syria.

Although Cook did not directly refer to the causes behind those battles which were performed in self-defense following series of assaults and intimidations and conspiracies made by the Pagans of Quraysh in Mecca and Jewish tribes in Medina, he referred to the Quranic verses which were revealed coincide with those battles justifying the waging of Jihad, such as:

> *Permission to fight against disbelievers is given to those who are fought against. Because they have been wronged; and surely, Allah is able to give the believers victory. Those who have been expelled from their homes unjustly only because they said: "Our Lord is Allah".* (22:39)

> *"For had it been not that Allah checks one set of people by means of another, monasteries, churches, synagogues and*

---

50 David Cook, Understanding Jihad, California University of California Press, 2005.

*mosques where in the Name of Allah is mentioned much
would surely, have been pulled down..." (22:40)*

Cook has highlighted concepts of Jihad and the regulations governing declaration of Jihad as well as distinguishing the greater Jihad from the Lesser Jihad. Cook fairly detailed the role of Jihad as a successful tool to respond to the crusades and Mongol invasions as well as its role in extending Muslim conquests to Spain and Central Asian countries including India where the conversions of Turks, Uzbeks and Mongols added large territories. Cook tracked all attempts of resistance against European conquests and even internal purification effort directed against Muslims by including the nineteenth century resistance in Palestine, Kashmir ...etc. as well as the recent global Islamist movements. Although in the light of Cook's assessment we may classify the history of Jihad into six stages:

- Battles and raids (Ghazwat) made during Prophet's Life and during the era of the four Caliphs.
- Battles of Ummaya and Abbasid.
- Battles of the Ottoman Empire.
- Individual resistance attempt of the nineteenth century under the Umbrella of Jihad.
- Contemporary fighting sponsored by global groups.

Study and evolution of Islamic Jihad – a concept known among all Muslims as the six pillar of Islam for fourteen centuries – in general may be misleading and rather incomprehensible. Since the 7th century the term Jihad as a victorious element was unfaithfully misused with different objectives and diverse policies. It was intentionally misused by governments and groups including even non-Muslims for multiple tasks. It is the duty of contemporary Muslim scholars to re-examine Jihad through the history to distinguish between the proper Jihad from the other patterns of invasions and raids. There is enough evidence concerning the practice of Jihad and well documented classical and contemporary works on Jihad, however, there is lack of new theories and interpretations of Jihad that might purify the image of Jihad. Admitting the centrality and importance of the theme of Jihad in Muslim civilization and faith of Islam, David Cook concluded his informative study with an equivocal remark, as follows:

1- "Today's Jihad movements are as legitimate as any that have ever existed in classical Islam with the exception of the fact that today's Jihad is lacking a legitimate authority such as Caliph or an Imam who could declare Jihad."

By reviewing this remark with Muslim scholars, it was found that the great majority disagree with Cook, because classical Jihad is the duty of the Islamic State represented by Caliph, Imam or president.

2- Cook raised vital questions;

First: Does the waging of military Jihad have future as a major theme in Islam? But his answer was negative, because Jihad has been a dismal failure during the past two centuries.

Second: Whether Jihad is primarily non-violent and superseded by spiritual Jihad and whether it is actually existing and superseding militant Jihad? The answer may be "yes", spiritual Jihad – the great Jihad – is the most visible in the daily life of Muslims. The daily five prayers, fasting, pilgrimage and self-control against many attractive things are spiritual Jihad, well known among the great majority of Muslims who has never practiced military Jihad. Thus, spiritual Jihad is the most significant element and would never disappear. The most critical and provocative remark made by Cook is that: "Since Muslims are no longer politically or militarily in the world, all implementation of the Sharia with ultimately collide with the non-Muslim world's norms (human rights). This can easily be seen by examining the four states that Sharia, such as Saudi Arabia, Afghanistan and Nigeria where domination of Sharia came under critical surveillance."

3. The theory of Anti-West

The theory of Anti-West recently advocated by several American scholars, has generated many critical reactions, giving unhealthy impact on public opinion in the United States of America and the Arab countries as well. The theory was not neither scientific nor Logical, because it was concluded from essays written to answer the question "Why do they hate us so much?" which appeared on the American academic scene, following the events of September,11. When such a vague question was raised in the light of September 11 tragedy, the American public began looking for the answer only within the Arab Muslim Communities, because, the perpetrators of September 11 events were only Arab Muslims. That was not the right question of that moment. Many scholars from U.S.A. and the Arab countries exchanged open letters of accusation and defense. Never the less those who really hate Americans were not involved in the deliberations related to the question.

Walter lacquer [51] attempted to answer the question by showing that nations and great powers are seldom loved. Neither Russia nor China nor India or Germany were loved, according to Walter, because big powers often tend to disregard the legitimate interests of smaller countries. This may be acceptable in case of the relation between the big nations and countries which may be in competition with America.

In fact, the great majority the Arabs are fond of America, and extremely bound with common interests. They love Americans and do respect them. The young generation in the Arab world consider American way of life, political and social system as a good model. The number of Arabs annually applying for the American green card lately is one simple evident, supporting such hypothesis.

The concept of Anti-Americanism is a myth, and its links with Jihad and terrorism may be groundless, if one could understand the real situation in the Arab Islamic countries. It is most difficult to guess what people love or hate, in the absence of freedom of expression. The

---

51 Walter Liqueur, Terrorism in the Twenty-First Century. New York, Continuum, 2004

Western community is making its judgments according to very limited voices from one side, and almost the same individuals who are repeating the same ideas during the last three or four decades. No. none in the Arab world- for instance – can demonstrate to support America or to say a word in its favor. The governments allow only Anti-American voices to tell America that, the public opinion is not in its favor. In fact, these are not the central issues pertaining to our subject, however, it is essential to understand that America is not hated by the majority of Arab Muslims. The great majority of Arab Muslim should not be blamed for the deeds of the very small terroristic groups, fighting under the umbrella of Jihad.

The majority of the Arab Muslims are innocent and peaceful and respectful to America and the West because they do appreciate what America and West are giving to the mankind.

The small groups of Arab Muslim Mujahidin are the results of misruling in some Arab countries, where new generations are grown under very critical political and socio- economic environment, it extremely difficult for the new generations of the internet era to understand what is happening in their communities. The will remain as terroristic groups because they are made by the governments, and sometimes encouraged and used by the West. Such groups of so called Arab Afghan Mujahidin including Abdullah Azzam and Usama Bin Laden and the rest were considered "freedom fighters" by the United States of America, which offered them even stinger antiaircraft missiles.[52]

4. Clash of civilizations and Jihad

Although Western Leaders, so-called moderate Arab Leaders and several politically-oriented scholars, apparently deny existence of any form of clash of civilizations, particularly between the western and the Islamic civilizations, we are of opinion that, there is a notable correlation between the objectives of Islamic Jihad and clash of civilizations. The clash of civilizations posited by Samuel Huntington is not a myth. It

---

52 Aukai Collins. My Jihad, Connecticut: The Lyons Press. 2002. P.9

is real and deeply rooted in history and well-highlighted by the basic Islamic sources, as well as religious sources.

In Huntington's theory civilization is "the broadest level of cultural identity" of and individual, ethnic group or nation and distinguishes three major ones: Western, Islamic-Arabic and Chinese. They may share certain values and over time may come to share more. But for the time being and for several generations, rather than just decades to come, the differences between them are "not only real, but basic". Certain Western values such as individualism, liberty, equality, tolerance, constitutional government, the rule of law, democracy, or free markets are not only found in the West; but fundamental commitment to them in combination certainly is. Not only the Taliban's Afghanistan, but numerous so-called moderate Arab/Islamic states and their regimes abhor, even criminalize, many of these value. Huntington also believes that the growth of fundamentalism, the ongoing "secularization" of many parts of the world, is by no means anywhere near a completed process. Cultural clashes will continue to proliferate.

Huntington was faithful and fair enough when he said[53]: "Whenever Islam will remain Islam – and there is no doubt in that – and whenever the West will remain the West – and no one is expecting that the West will become East- the clash will remain as it has been since fourteen centuries.

The great majority of the well-educated Arab and Muslim scholar were not surprised by Huntington's theory of clash of civilizations of 1993, because, the basic roots of clash of civilizations were well maintained in Islamic sources and within the works of contemporary Muslim scholars.

Before, five decades or more, Sayed Qutb outlined the probable cause of clash between Islam and the Western culture. In his famous book titled "Maalim Fi Al-Tarig" Qutb states:

---

53 Samuel Huntington, The Clash of Civilizations and the Remaking of the world order. London, Simon & Schuster, 19979

"There is sever conflict between two ideas, two concepts, two communities, two systems and two facts. Islam on one side and disbelieve, right and wrong, evil and good, rule of Allah and rule of human beings, Allah and Tacghoot. Therefore, there is no existence for one without eradicating the other. There is no way for reconciliation or agreement. Change should take place by revolution and not gradually.... The contemporary situation is in basic conflict with the Islamic way of life and concepts of Islam. It deprives us by force our right to live as we like according to Islamic rules without changing our values. We are at road cross".

Sayed Qutb statement may be supported also by the Qur'anic verse which says:

"Never will the Jews nor the Christians be pleased with you (O Muhammed) till you follow their religion. Say verily the guidance of Allah, that is the only guidance. And if you were to follow their guidance after what you have received of knowledge, then you would have against Allah neither any protector nor any helper" (1:120).

The western scholars were very far from the Islamic movements began following the 1st. world war and reached its peak after the 2nd. World war. Western scholars and politicians emphasizing their political and economic targets in the Islamic world has ignored the process of the rapid revitalization of Islamic teachings took placing at that time. The abundance literature produced by well-educated Muslims scholars has clearly stated the contradicting principles and in Islam and western cultures. That is why western scholars of today are attempting to deny the theory of Huntington. This is obvious, when Benjamin Barber, the author of Jihad Vs. Mc world says, "Bin Laden is the primary Biblicist for Huntington's theory. For Huntington a clash of civilizations was a worst-case scenario. For Bin Laden it was a game plane."

In fact, Bin Laden was one of many renewals of religion who appear in Islamic history from time to time. He was some publicists for the original Islamic principle and teachings highlighted by the Muslim scholars of mid-twenties century, such as Hassen Al-Benna, Sayed. Qutob, Mohamed Abdu, Mohamed Abdul Wahab, Mohamed Ahmed El Mahadi…etc.

In March 1928, Hassan al-Banna founded the Muslim brother hood. Inspired by Jamal ad-Din al-Afghani (1839-1897) the ideological father of the 20th. Century Islamic movement. and Muhammed Abdu (1849-1905).

Sayyed Qutb book (Fi Zilal al-Qur'n) in the shadow of the Qur'an and Maalim fi-al-Tariq (signposts on the Road), had developed the concepts of the original Islam (the salafi) to distinguish between the original Muslim Umma and those whom he identified as infidel barbarism. In Qutb's view (jahiliyah) includes everything that leis outside the original Islam including secularist rulers and scholars of Islamic countries.

Francis Fukuyama, one of the most writers critical to Huntington's theory, assesses Huntington thesis as follows:

> "It had a mischievous impact on the way people around the world thought about these things. It is not just wrong; it is also not helpful to world politics. It gives aid and comfort to people who want to reject Western Values".

However, Fukuyama who has rejected Huntington's theory, was more helpless to the world politics and more provocative for Muslims when he wrote his "The End of History" in 1989. Fukuyama wrote:

> "What we may in fact be witnessing," he wrote, "is not just the passing of a particular period of postwar history, but the end point of mankind's ideological evolution and the emergence of Western liberal democracy as the final form of human government. Borrowing the

vocabulary of Hegel and Marx, it may be the end of history. The end of history will be a very sad time. In the post-historical period, there will be neither politics nor philosophy."

Concluding the history of mankind with the prevalence of Western Values and superiority of Western cultures, as stated by Fukuyama was disappointing for many Muslims and rather provocative to others who felt that the West is threatening the Islamic culture. Fukuyama's statements were added to the facts that gave ground for Islamic Jihad revivalisms.

Islamic culture is very rich. If Muslim scholars can understand the objectives of the original Islamic sources in the context of the contemporary globalization trends, they may be able to contribute in the well faire of mankind, provided that they take in consideration the favorable Western values. The West may not be able to take Islamic values. However, Muslims have a chance to enjoy their own values plus the most attractive values known in the West namely, freedom, democracy and justice and fairness. In the free society sponsored by the West real Islam will spread because it's spiritual, effective and system of life. Jihad not exist but Jihad by wisdom and reasoning will gain more and contribute.

SIX

FINAL ANALYSES AND REMARKS

1 – Final analyses

The new peak of the contemporary violence and terroristic war began in October 1981, when Egyptian resident Anwar Al- Sadat was assassinated by a group of the Egyptian Armed Forces led by lt. Khalid Al-Istanabouli, a member of Al-jihad. Al-Sadat assassination was followed by series of exchanged massacres between Algerian army and the militants of the Islamic Salvation Front which was facing the Algerian Army Crackdown only because (ISF) had won in a free democratic election. In the 1990s US military was attacked in Riyadh and Dhahran. Again in 1998, American embassies in Tanzania and Kenya were bombed. The worst of such terroristic war was of course 11 September 2001 and the case of Iraq, which created a wide-open adverbial relationship between Muslims and the Western nations in general, and particularly United States of America, which went into declared war against an unknown target, giving opportunity to others who may characterizes its war against terrorism itself as terrorism.

In this context, it seems to any reasonable man, that international terrorism remains as a critical challenge facing the whole settings of the contemporary world. Issues related to terrorism, such as defining terrorism, distinction between terrorism and Jihad or fighting for freedom, causative factors of terrorism and international cooperation in combating terrorism remain only as an academic works. In this research, attempts made to revive such issues has generated the following analyses:

1. **Distinction between Jihad and terrorism:**

Perhaps, without considering the above themes it may not be possible to distinguish between Jihad and terrorism. However, it might be argued that there is no need for a definition of terrorism if one deals with it as a criminal act, whatever the means and whoever employs it. Indeed, the consequences of acts of terror and violence are common crimes in every civilized nation. Therefore, an exact legal definition is not necessary if one merely deals with the element of the *actus rues* (conduct) in question, such as murder, serious bodily injuries, sabotage, exploding properties, hostage taking or hijacking.[54] However, for the purpose of drawing distraction between contemporary patterns of terrorism and Islamic Jihad, the following definitions may be considered.

Given the rise in what appears to be Islamic related terrorism, many scholars have begun to explore the links between terrorism and the concept of Islamic Jihad. Much of this analysis, especially in the West, is informed by ideological perspectives that are antagonistic towards Islam.

Given the above definitions (and similar) which are illustrated by the incidents of violence we are witnessing today throughout the world, it is becoming easier to understand the elements and factors of any terroristic activity. However, to emphasize the distinction between terrorism and Islamic Jihad, we shall summarize the key elements of difference in table 1.

---

54 Friedlander, R.A., "Terrorism and International Law: recent Development" Rutgers Law Journal 13 (1982) P. 450.

Table1: a summary of the comparison between Jihad and Terrorism

Characteristics of	
Terrorism	**Jihad**
1. Committed by clandestine groups.	1. Performed by Muslims organized and directed by official authorities of an identified Islamic nation.
2. Politically motivated.	2. Motivated by religion.
3. Violence and sabotage.	3. May be by tongue, heart or use of force.
4. Against combatant or non-combatant targets.	4. Against combatant and identified groups.
5. With the intention of influencing an audience or propagandize claim.	5. With the intention of gaining Allah's reward and paradise.
6. Victims and targets are selected, however, beyond the selected targets, there are random victims and targets.	6. Civilians, children, women and old people should not be victimized.
7. Targets include buildings, public properties, means of transportation…etc.	7. Buildings and properties should not be targeted.
8. Any type of weapons and means of destruction may be used.	8. Only weapons similar to that of the enemy may be used.
9. Muslims and scriptural are victimized.	9. No Jihad against Muslims.
10. A sudden activity.	10. Declared fighting.

2 - Controversial views of Muslim scholars

To review the previously discussed controversial opinions of Muslim scholars and Islamic groups, a survey was conducted among a number of authorized Muslim scholars so as to:

- Develop a popular concept of Islamic Jihad.
- Adoption of a uniform understanding of the issue, rules and guidelines of Jihad.
- Distinguish Islamic Jihad as a religious practice and worship, far away from the contemporary violence characterized as terrorism.
- To outline future objectives of Jihad and adoption of means to realize such objectives in a manner that maintains Jihad as one of the respectable pillars of Islam.

In furtherance of this survey, a questionnaire was sent to (1300) Muslim scholars and writers in (38) Islamic countries. In addition, the published works, statements, interviews, and published advisory opinions of (15) Muslim scholars were also considered within this survey. The questions were arranged to understand the opinion of the Muslim scholars on specific patterns of contemporary acts of violence performed by the clandestine groups as well as the acts of those who are fighting for freedom or self-defense under the umbrella of Islamic Jihad. The questions included the uprising in Palestine, suicide operations; terroristic activities in Islamic countries, fighting in Iraq or Afghanistan, and fighting on behalf of unelected governments to suppress the rebelling forces, September, 11 attacks, principles and future of Jihad. (890) of the scholars responded to the questionnaire.

After a careful examination of the answers and comments of the respondents we have concluded the following indications:

- According to all of the responding scholars, Jihad is an everlasting obligation of every Muslim until the Day of Resurrection.
- According to 66% responding scholars, Jihad should continue against the disbelievers, if they threaten Muslims' religion or expel the Muslims from their lands.
- According to 97% of the sample scholars, Jihad should be declared and organized by an Islamic government, but not by individuals.

- 66% of the sample considers Jihad an individual Muslims' responsibility, if there is no Islamic government or caliph to take the leadership responsibility.
- According to 89% of the sample fighting against foreigners who invade or conquer Muslims' lands, is a typical form of Jihad and obligatory for every Muslim.
- According to 98% of the sample Palestinians' upraise "Intifada" is Jihad, because they were expelled from their land.
- 23% of the sample considers September, 11, 2001 as a form of Jihad, because there was a declared war between America and Al-Qaeda.
- 84% of the sample considers fighting against the present rulers of the Islamic countries as a political violence, but not Jihad.
- According to 83% of the sample, fighting those who commit armed robberies is Jihad.
- According to 31% of the sample fighting to support Muslim minorities in foreign countries is Jihad, and duty upon every individual Muslim.
- According to 92% of the sample, the present governments of the Islamic Countries should not be targets of Jihad, because they are Muslim leaders and maintaining Islamic rules.
- According to all of the responding scholars the terroristic incidents, which were committed in Islamic Countries and killing civilian non-Muslims were not Jihad.
- According to 76% of the sample fighting the foreign forces occupying Iraq, Afghanistan, Chechnya, is Jihad.

3 - The strategy of Fatwa's:

Promoting Fatwa's and publishing statements condemning terrorism was sponsored by governments participating in war against terrorism as one of the strategies in facing Al Qaeda Jihad, since September 11, 2001.

In Hajj ceremony of February 2, 2004, Sheikh Abdul Aziz Abdallah Al Sheikh, Chief Mufti of the Saudi Arabian Kingdom, condemning Extremism and enhancing Moderation has stated:[55]

> "You must know Islam's firm position against all these terrible crimes. The world must know that Islam is a religion of peace and mercy and goodness; it is a religion of justice and guidance… Islam has forbidden violence in all its forms. It forbids hijacking airplanes, ships and other means of transport, and it forbids all acts that undermine the security of the innocent people."

Similar fatwa's and statements were being issued in different occasions by Muslims Sheikhs, clerics, scholars and political leaders, condemning crimes of violence and terrorism and killing innocent people. Among those who issued fatwas were scholars and Sheikhs from all over the world including prominent figures such as:

- Sheikh Saleh Al Luheidan.
- Sheikh Muhammad Bin Abdullah Sabil.
- Sheikh Yusuf Al Qaradawi.
- Mehmet Nuri Yilmaz.
- Harun Yahya.
- Sheikh Muhammad Yusuf Islahi.
- Abdal Hahim Murad.
- Sayed Mumtaz Ali.
- American Muslim Organizations.
- Leaders of North American Muslim Organizations.
- President Muhammad Khatami.
- League of Arab States.
- General Secretary of the Organization of the Islamic Conference.
- Hamza Yusuf.
- Yusuf Islam.
- Professor Muqtedan Khan.

---

55 www.saudiembassy.net/report.

- Dr. Alaa Al Yusuf.
- Dr. S.Pravez Manzoor.
- Ziauddin Sardar.
- Khalid Abu El Fadl.
- Sheikh Muhammad Ali Al Hanooti.
- Sayed Shahabuddin.
- Dr. M.A. Zaki Badawi.
- Mufti Nizamuddin Shamzai.
- Sheikh Omar Bakri.
- Zuhair Qudah.
- Sheikh Rashid Al Ghannoushi.
- Sheikh Salih Al Suhaymi.
- Dr. Sayed Safari.
- Iqbal Siddiqui.
- Islamic Commission of Spain.
- Fatwa of 500 British Scholars and clerics.

Considering all words and expressions of condemnation included in the above mentioned fatwa's and statements, we could hardly single-out a fatwa that tells us about Jihad and the justification of the causes behind those terroristic activities as all edged by the extremists and their sympathizers. The extremists are claiming that there is a declared war between two parties. There is a declared war from several non-Muslim countries against terrorism. They consider war against terrorism a war against a war against the radical Islamists. However, who are the Islamists. Of course they are Muslims. Anyone who claims that he is Muslim may easily gain support of other Muslims. Extremists are now calling new generations with carefully selected Quranic verses, as well as reasoning, while others are silent or just propagating political slogans. Motivating Jihad and indoctrinating those who are politically and socially handicapped is advancing. New methods and technologies of preaching, recruiting and on-line training are considered —according to the radicals- as practical miracles in the Cause of Allah.

* The Impact of fatwa:

Re-calling such innumerable fatwa's and condemnation statements issued by Muslims scholars and Sheikhs during the last decade, it may be relevant to examine the results and impact of such literature exposed through a global effective mass-media.

In the light of our limited investigations and analysis, several notable facts were obtained:

- Fatwas and condemnation statements could hardly gain the respect of the public in the Islamic countries, where people has taken such fatwa's as decrees serving interests of the un-elected governments and having nothing to do with Islam —as religion, or the citizens' urgent interests.
- Despite such numerous fatwa's and statements, the radical Muslims went away with their strategies of violence and attacks against the targets they have chosen.
- On the other hand, the moderate Muslims' attitude revealed by such fatwa's and statements does not brighten Islam's image in the eyes of the Westerners. It appears that fatwa's and condemnations were just for political objectives.
- Fatwas were not popular, issued in isolation, spread in darkness.
- Fatwas has condemned killing innocent people and emphasized Islam's justice, its rejection of violence and terrorism. They have used the same terms and issues claimed by Islamist. The issue of Jihad was absolutely ignored by Sheikhs and clerics who made the statements.
- Muslim scholars and non- Muslim scholars are talking with different languages. Muslims condemn terrorism, but not Jihad, while non- Muslims do not differentiate between Jihad and terrorism. So for successful communication let us address Jihad.
- Addressing Muslim people in religious issues requires religious methodology. That means we need acceptable models of clerics and Sheikhs rather than official ones. A faithful cleric or sheikh,

who can talk righteous religion rather than unpopular politics, is needed to guide Muslims against Al Qaeda sheikhs.

4 – Monopoly of Fatwas

The dilemma facing Muslim scholars today is not only to claim the absence of the term terror in the main sources of Islam, but also to explain the concept of Jihad which is repeatedly affirmed by the Holy Quran, and to prove that Islamic Jihad is not a model of contemporary terrorism. Contemporary Muslim scholars are almost all influenced by the governments and political parties, and in consequence their span of analyses and Fatwas tend to be limited due to political influence and pressures imposed by different political authorities and religious factions, who are prepared to issue decrees that might disqualify any Muslim scholar who attempts to raise issues outside of a narrow perspective. Recently, voices were raised against what is known as Fatwa monopoly in Saudi Arabia. In a preparatory workshop for the 5th National Dialogue Form, Saudi Intellectuals called for an end to the monopoly of Islamic propagation and held the religious curricula responsible for the struggle and hatred against the "others".

Lubna Al Ansari, a Saudi female scholar, criticized the monopolization of Islamic propagation by certain groups, wrote:

> "as if the call for Islam is limited to them only. This trend contradicts the teachings of the Quran and the Prophet Mohammad (PBUH)."

Dr. Hatoon Al Fasy, another female scholar, stressed the importance of respecting different ideologies, she says:

> "We should recognize that we have many ideologies, and that there are some differences among these ideologies".

The recommendations issued by the workshop said the pioneering role of Saudi Arabia entails that it adopts a moderate method. The deliberations of the workshop concentrated on the best means of dealing with "others" in accordance with Islamic Sharia. Some participants condemned attempts by some scholars in Saudi Arabia to monopolize fatwa (Islamic decree) and said this monopolization should come to an end. They said some signs of hatred witnessed among the people in Saudi society against non-Muslims could be attributed to this monopolization. Mohammad Bin Nasser Al Asmari, a Saudi writer and journalist, referring to the history textbook of secondary school, said the curricula are responsible for implanting hatred in the hearts of young people.

The workshop stressed the importance of increasing public awareness on the political side of globalization and on the spread of common political values. The intellectuals, in their recommendations, called for openness towards the cultures of other societies and to maintain relations based on reciprocal trust. "Attention should be given to the means that support good relations with other people and to develop this trend for the benefit of mankind in general," said the recommendations.

The participants exchanged accusations against each other without mentioning specific names. Some made a link between the terrorist attacks against the US on September 11, 2001, and some articles by Saudi writers instigating the perpetrators to commit these attacks[1].

2 – Conclusions and remarks

Islam is not only an ideology or philosophy maintained by humankind, but it is a religion of Allah, deeply rooted in the hearts and minds of more than one billion throughout the world. The Quran, The Holy Book of all Muslims is not a work of human. It is the words of Allah, who revealed it to his messenger Muhammad, with a promise of guarding it until the last day of this life. For those who learn the Arabic Language, the Quran is of great psychological and spiritual impact. It is an everlasting source of behavior and spiritual power. Therefore, confronting Muslims through their religious belief may not be in favor of the global peace and security. Any attempt of war against Islam or Islamic teachings may generate more fanatic Muslims, claiming Jihad as a religious obligation. However:

- According to the sharia definition of Jihad and the advisory opinions of Muslim scholars, the recent incidents of violence and terroristic activities should not be classified as Jihad.

- Islamic Jihad is governed by clear principle and guidelines. It is fighting for Allah's cause, declared by well-known authorities of an Islamic state for specific targets and causes.

- Treating Islamic Jihad issues should not be through similar strategies adopted to face terrorism.

- The problems surrounding containment of Jihad and Mujahedeen is due to the poor knowledge of Islam and the governmental efforts of Islamic states in fighting them only through security measures.

- This new trend of the leader of Egyptian Islamic groups is a positive step towards modern understanding of Jihad in the context of globalization. It is an attempt to bridge the gap between Muslim scholars and western scholar, such trend should be supported by the national and regional governments as well as the international community. The reaction of the international community to this repentance of Islamic groups should be more effective. The governmental and intergovernmental organizations should encounter the new step with more social, political and psychological effort. Democracy, freedom of expression, justice and equity, as well as reformation of the completely social and political settings are most urgent.

- Muslim jurists and independent Muslim scholars must clarify the well-rooted Islamic teachings as standing sources of Jihad such as:

    o Believers performing Jihad are superior-before Allah than those believers who are performing other various kinds of worship.

    o Jihad as fighting in Allah's cause was forbidden at the beginning of Prophet Muhammad's mission, then it was permitted and later it was made obligatory against those who worship others along with Allah or those who expel Muslims from their homes.

- Those who lead, invite, abet others for Jihad and support "Mujahidin" with wealth and weapons are also given equal rewards as Jihad doers.
- To prepare well-trained troops and maintain weapons and strong fighting forces is obligatory[56]. Therefore, Muslims have no reason to abandon Jihad.

In reviewing the worsening relationship between Muslims and the non-Muslims in the west, there is an obvious demarcation between the positions of the governments of the Islamic countries on one hand and the people on the other hand. Moreover, it is essential to appreciate and support the great majority of Muslims who are not involved in terrorism or politics in general, to shift them from their passive or neutral position to the side of global antiterrorism campaign. The great majority of Muslims are far away from the reins of political powers in their countries. Therefore, no dialogue will be fruitful between the Islamic countries and non-Muslim countries, unless the great majority of Muslims are involved. Lack of fair dialogue between the two parties will leave the great majority of Muslims at large, and free of any commitments of their un-elected governments. Distinguished Muslim scholars began to turn cause of failure inward on Muslims, due to the misinterpretation of the idea of rectitude in Islamic countries. It may be unfair to take any action or inflect any punishment by the international community on those citizens who has never been in power or practiced decision making in their respective countries. Therefore, as noted by Feldman[57], the single most pressing question of today is that whether democracy can be an alternative for the present Jihad dilemma.

The answer is simply yes. Real democracy and the western pattern of freedom of expression is the only way to reshape the Islamic world

---

56 In this context, many Muslim scholars consider Nuclear weapons as one of the sources of force to be procured by Muslims to the extent that their enemies procure this weapon.

57 Noah Feldman, After Jihad, American and struggle for Islamic Democracy. New York: Farrar straus &Giroux,2004.

to cope with the international community. Democracy will make the Muslims to choose their right path in the context of the international law. There is no evidence now to say, that the great majority of Muslims are behind Jihad and fighting for the cause of Allah. Is majority with the contemporary Mujahedeen or against? Is the majority backing the Palestine problem or not?

In a democratic Islamic country, Muslims may decide what fairly on realistic Islamic teachings without fear.

Through free dialogue, Muslims may be able to solve their own conflicts first. New and appropriate interpretations of Quran and Sunna may emerge, if there is freedom. Muslims will be able to reshape the image of Islam according to their common interests and religious objectives, because Islam is suitable for all generations of the humankind. It is notable that Muslim scholars have a limited freedom of thinking. They are always under threats from the politicians and the fanatic groups as well. Muslims' uniform understanding of Islamic Jihad may open doors for fruitful dialogue with the international community and the non-Muslims throughout the world to re-examine Islam and Muslims and take a fair judgements. Thereafter, if any freely elected government in any country attempts to preform Jihad in a way that might affect international peace and security, it will be the right of the international community to apply international laws. There, the theory of state responsibility may emerge on fair grounds.

Again, Muslim scholars are also exploring arguments to prove the innocence of Islam from any terroristic accusations. For instance, according to Shukri[58], in the Quran, the Arabic terms "Rahba" meaning terror and its derivatives appears eight times, and only once it is used in the sense of scaring the enemies of Allah and the believers during "Jihad". This is stated in the Quranic Verse, which reads as follows:

> *"Against them make ready your strength to the utmost of your powers including steeds of war to strike terror into the hearts of the enemies of Allah and your enemies."* (8:60).

---

58 Muhammad Aziz Shukri, International Terrorism: A Legal Critique. Vermont: Amana Books, 1991.

In the other seven instances as quoted by Shukri, "Rahba" is used solely to call for the fear of Allah. Although this is one of the most annoying verses for the non- Muslims, Shukri could not explain the objectives and dimensions of the above Quranic Verse. Moreover, for non-Muslims terrorism is not limited only to the word terror. There are terms of fighting for the cause of Allah, fight the disbelievers, kill them…. etc. mentioned in Quran, ought to be thoroughly interpreted by Muslim scholars today.

Considering the above views, we may draw four broad themes for discussion:

Firstly; Islam as a religion and its teachings and principles are well accepted and appreciated even by disbelievers throughout the world. There is no need to be apologetic about Islam.

Secondly, many Muslim scholars repeatedly emphasize Islamic rules, principles, guidelines as most appropriate to organize human behavior and realize justice and social well fair. However, in this respect they draw on models of the very old Islamic history. They never discuss the present situation of the Muslims. They avoid the contemporary behavior of Muslims that is of course the concern of the international community. Today, there is no specific Islamic state or community that can be taken as a successful guiding module to encourage other communities to follow the same.

Why Muslims of today are so different from their historical ancestors? Why do they tend to violence? Why do they hate others? Why Muslims of today are classified into extremists, fanatics and secularists? Who is authorized speak on behalf of Muslims? Who is responsible for the deteriorating psychological, political, social and economic situation of Muslims, in the Islamic countries in particular and throughout the world in general? Many such questions remain without answer, as a cause of depression and hate.

Thirdly, there are problems related to the definition of Islamic States their existence and their realities in the context of the modern global system and legality. In this respect, most controversial is the issue of the relations between the present ruling regimes of the so called

Islamic States and their citizens? What is the current Islamic States' responsibility for the behavior of the individuals?

Following the 2nd World War, Islamic countries developed a controversial or unacceptable pattern of political and religious leadership. Perhaps, that was due to political and socio-economic factors. Notably. the support of the Western industrial countries to such political systems was of great impact in creation of contemporary regimes. Consequently, Muslims have lost a uniform and acceptable religious authority that organizes and controls the general behavior of the new generation in the Islamic states. Accordingly, innumerable leaders and unqualified Muslim scholars have emerged. Individuals are practicing interpretation of Qur'an and issuing legal advice as "fatwa" in most critical religious issues. Notably, calling for Jihad within the Islamic countries and against the disbelievers has been emphasized by such groups and politically oriented religious factions.

Accordingly, it is urgent task to develop the political and socio-economic settings in the Islamic communities. It is essential to make pathway for new political and religious leaders who have the capacity to conciliate between Islamic teachings and the requirements of the contemporary international legality, and avoid internal and external conflicts. We need exemplary Islamic leaders that stand as peacemakers and settle disputes between Muslims before they generate violence.

Fourthly, who are the disbelievers in the Islamic perspective and who are the enemies of Islam, against whom Muslims are asked to fight for Allah's Cause? Who is supposed to sponsor Jihad in the absence of Islamic state? Is it open to every individual to call for Jihad and sponsor "Mujahedeen", as well as selecting the targets of Jihad?

Feldman suggests democratization of Islamic states as a workable strategy to turn Muslims from political violence to participate in electoral politics; with the historical roots of democracy available in Islam.

So, contrary to what is believed in the US; Islam is not inherently committed to the overthrow of Western ideals. To the contrary, many though by no means all, Muslims find the combination of Islamic ideals and democratic values appealing. Today Muslims around the world embrace the elegance, logic, and depth of Islam perhaps more warmly than at any time in a century. In Islam's language of justice, morality, hope, and commitment, they find not only religion, but a vital force in the realms of politics, society, and the spirit. At the same time, as their reliance on Islam grows, Muslims are also embracing the ideals of self-government and freedom associated with democracy. To an increasing number of Muslims, these democratic values resonate with Islam and can develop in tandem with it. Wherever advocates have been free to speak out or run for office in the name of Islamic democracy, they have found an eager audience.

Feldman, however, seems to be anxious about the reality of the future of Islamic democracy and its impact on the great majority of Muslims upon whom strict religious dictates of Islamic law might be enforced through policing of personal religious practices. In fact, democracy is democracy whatever it is the religion of the voters. If democracy is practiced in an Islamic society, no doubt it will reflect Islamic values in the context of the modern global environment. Democracy is not new in history, but the mechanism may be improved to meet the needs of the present Islamic communities.

Noah Feldman, professor at New York University with a doctorate degree in Islamic Thought from Oxford has dealt with issue of Jihad in a unique and rather constructive way. Feldman, understanding the way of thinking of many moderate Muslims, wrote his book titled; after Jihad: America and the struggle for Islamic Democracy[59](1). The Prophet, upon whom be prayers and peace, was returning from one of their battles, when he said, "you have made the finest of returns; you have returned from the lesser Jihad to the greater Jihad." They said, "and what is the greater Jihad?" he answered, "Man's struggle against his desires."

Starting his work with the above famous words of Prophet Muhammad – prayers and peace be upon him – Feldman attempted to call for encouraging the great majority of the moderate Muslims to enhance causes of the greater Jihad as a means to overcome the growing ideology of violence, attributed to Jihad:

---

59 Noah Feldman. After Jihad: America and the struggle for Islamic Democracy, New York, Farra, Straus and Giroux.2003.

"There are still some people prepared to do violence in the name of Islam, who will doubtless make continued attempts to terrorize the West. But many, perhaps most, Muslims are, instead, entering a confirmed period of post-Jihad, "post" in the sense that the option of holy war now seems spent, peripheral, unrealistic, and indeed distasteful in the light of the violence of September11. They are turning toward another kind of Jihad that is embedded in Islamic thought and tradition, a type of Jihad explicated in the well-known hadith that forms the epigraph. In one version of this received tradition, Prophet Muhammad has delivered sobering message: "you have returned from the lesser Jihad to embark upon the greater Jihad". In the orthodox interpretation of the anecdote, incorporated in some versions of the tradition, the greater Jihad is the inward struggle to perfect one's moral qualities. Sufi mystics have long embraced this interpretation, which they extend to mean that life's central task lies in overcoming the ego.

More broadly, inward Jihad is a worthy struggle infused by the principles of religion. One might say it was this more general type of struggle that Prophet described as the greater Jihad, as opposed to the lesser Jihad of actual war. Jihad can also mean, then, by association, Islam's struggle to create a just system of political government. After all, the Muslims whom the Prophet addressed were returning to the bosom of their community, presumably to take up its affairs".

Finally, in my opinion, it is not possible to generate a uniform understanding of Jihad and fighting for the cause of Allah by the Muslims.

It is not possible to amend the Quran; however, it is possible to interpret Quran to suit every place and every era.

The only possible and practical solution is a call for an International conference on this topic to adopt an international convention on combating fighting for a religious cause.

REFERENCES

1. Alex Schmid, "Terrorism the Definitional Problem", Case Western Reserve Journal of International Law, Vol. 36, 2004.

2. Benjamin R. Barber, Jihad vs Mc World Terrorism's Challenge to Democracy. London: A Corgi Book, 2003.

3. Bruce Hoffman, "Al Qaeda, Trends in Terrorism, and Future Potentialities: An Assessment." Studies in Conflict & Terrorism, Taylor & Francis, 26, 2003.

4. David Cook, Understanding Jihad. Berkeley: University of California Press, 2005.

5. Friedlander, R. A., "Terrorism and International Law: Recent Development" Rutgers Law Journal 13 (1982) P. 450.

6. Gilles Keppel, Jihad – The Trail of Political Islam, London: I.B.Tauris, 2004.

7. Harun Yahya, Islam Denounces Terrorism. Istanbul: Arastrima Publishing, 2002.

8. Jason Burke, Al-Qaeda: The True Story of Radical Islam. London: Penguin Books, 2004.

9. Justin Winkle, The Rough Guide: History of Islam. London: Penguin Books, 2003.

10. Mahmoud Sherif Bassiouni, United Nations, Intergovernmental Meetings of the Experts, Vienna, 14-18 March 1988.

11. Maxwell Taylor, The Fanatics: A behavioral approach to Political Violence. Exeter: Brassy's, 1991.

12. Mohamed Al Mamoon Al Hudhaiby, Arab New, News Paper No. 1041, issued Oct. 3rd, 2003.

13. Mohammed Aziz Shukri, International Terrorism: A legal critique. Vermont: Amana Books, 1991.

14. Noah Feldman, After Jihad: America and the Struggle for Islamic Democracy. New York: Farrar, Straus and Girouk, 2004.

15. Noorani A. G. Islam & Jihad: Prejudice Versus Reality. London: Zed Books, 2002.

16. Rex A. Hudson, "Dealing with International Hostage Taking", Terrorist Volume No. 221, London, 1983.

17. Samuel P. Huntington. The Clash of Civilizations and The Remarking of World Order. London: Simon & Schuster, 2002.

18. A Rage for order: The Middle East in Turmoil, from Tahrir square to ISIS, by Robert F. Worth, 2016,

19. Black Flags: The Rise of ISIS, by Joby Warrik, 2015

20. Defeating: The Wimble War, by Sebastian Gorka, 2016

21. They Say We Are Infidels: On The Run From ISIs with persecuted Christians in the Middle East, by Mindy Belz, 2016

22. The Looming Towers: Al- Qaeda and the Road to 9/11, by Lawrence Wright, 2007

23. It is About Islam: Exposing the Truth About ISIS, Al Qaeda, Iran, and the Caliphate, by Glenn Beck, 2015

24. Inside Terrorism, by Bruce Hoffman, 2006

25. Understanding Terrorism: Challenges, Perspectives and issues, by Clarence Augustus Martin, 2015

26. Terrorism Today: The Past, The Players, The Future, By Jeremy R. Spin love and Clifford Simon Sen, 2013

27. Terrorism in the Twenty- First Century, by Cynthia C. Combs, 2012

28. The Syrian Jihad: Al-Qaeda, the Islamic State and the Evolution of and Insurgency

29. The New Arad Wars: Uprising and Anarchy in the Middle East. By Marc Lynch, 2016-06-21 radical Islam Why? By Jeffrey F. Addicott. 2015

30. Islam and Politics, by Peter Mandeville, 2014

31. The Encyclopedia of Militant Islam by Bryan Griffin, 2016

32. www.Islam-online.net

33. www.jcpa.org

34. www.mediamonitors.net

35. www.Memri.org

36. www.saudiembassy.net

37. www.ummah.net

المراجـــــع:

1. ابن ماجه.2.

أحمد عبد الله، جمال البنا، صفي الدين حامد، أحمد عثمان، زغلول النجار، عصام العريان، ميرال الطحاوي وآخرون. قارعة سبتمبر، القاهرة: مكتبة الشروق الدولية ، 2002.

3. الإمام الأكبر/ محمد سيد طنطاوي، بنو إسرائيل في القرآن والسنَّة، القاهرة: دار الشروق، 2000، ص ص 745- 748.

4. الترمذي.

5. النسائي.

6. صحيح البخاري.

7. صحيح مسلم.

8. عمر القراي، الجهاد أم حرية الاعتقاد ، 1995.

9. كاساني، بدائع الصنائع.

10. كرم محمد زهدي – تفجيرات الرياض: الأحكام والآثار، القاهرة، 2003.

11. محمد خير هيكل، الجهاد والقتال في الإسلام في السياسة الشرعية، بيروت: دار البيارق 1993.

12. نهر الذكريات: المراجعة الفقهية للجماعة الإسلامية.